UN SHAKE ABLE

From Limiting Beliefs to Limitless Confidence and Empowerment

GOLDEN BOOK AWARDS

INTERNATIONAL AUTHOR WINNER 2025 EXCELLENCE AWARD

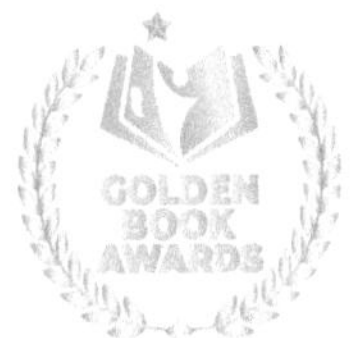

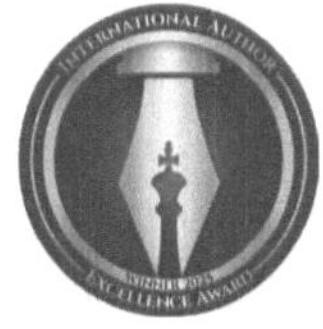

A JOURNEY TO REBUILD CONFIDENCE,
STRENGTHEN SELF-ESTEEM,
AND SHAPE A NEW FUTURE

SHABNAM OMER

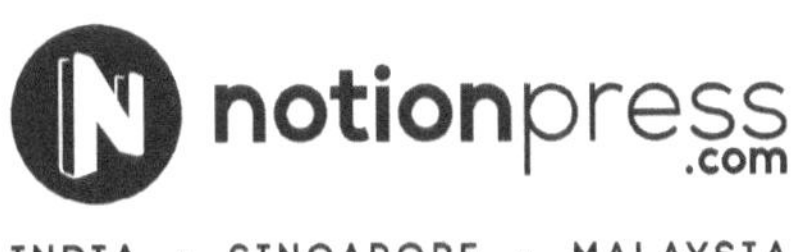

notionpress.com

INDIA • SINGAPORE • MALAYSIA

ISBN
Hardcase 979-8-89588-926-8
Paperback 979-8-89544-897-7

*This book is dedicated to my father, the late Omer Sait,
who has always motivated and supported me,
and to my mother, Zeenath Omer,
for her constant support.
My two daughters Muneerah Khan and Siya A,
and my niece Manaal Khan for believing in me
and encouraging me to follow my passion;
my siblings for their constant support and encouragement;
and my mentors,
without whom I would not have achieved my dreams.*

CONTENTS

Chapter 5

How do you enhance your self-esteem?   **68**

AUTHOR'S NOTE

My dear reader,

I'm pleased to welcome you to my book **Unshakeable: "A Journey to Rebuild Confidence, Strengthen Self-esteem, and Shape a New Future"**. My journey with self-esteem has always been wavering with ups and downs. As a child, I was unhappy, as I missed many good opportunities due to low self-esteem. Though I had the potential, I hadn't realised it.

Being in the counselling and coaching profession for more than two decades, I've encountered many individuals of different age groups and statuses struggling with low self-esteem, which has become the biggest roadblock for them to achieve their goals. Not only this, it leads to emotional distress, impacting their emotional and mental health drastically.

As a single parent, it was quite upsetting to see my daughters suffering with low self-esteem and comparing themselves to others. Today, they have grown into strong individuals with adequate self-esteem and are doing well in life. These personal experiences motivated me to write this book to help struggling people develop adequate self-esteem and achieve success and happiness.

Unshakeable is a book based on my life experience and my client's experiences. I have helped thousands of people overcome their low self-esteem and see a ray of hope in their lives. They succeeded in enhancing self-awareness, replacing their negative thoughts with positive ones, altering their mindset, becoming resilient, and achieving realistic goals leading to a happy and fulfilling life.

I sincerely hope that my book will be a game-changer for anyone trying to overcome their low self-esteem, enabling them to overcome their limiting beliefs, gain confidence, and manifest their dreams.

I genuinely believe that my story, real-life examples, stories, practical tips, strategies, and techniques in this book will have a positive impact on your mindset and help you become the best version of yourself, enabling you to live a happy and fulfilling life and achieve your dreams.

Please accept my sincere gratitude for allowing me to be a part of your journey.

Warm regards,

Shabnam Omer

PREFACE

In our life's journey, most of us encounter obstacles and easily give up, losing hope and accepting defeat; others overcome the challenges and adversities and succeed in achieving their dreams. Have you ever wondered why this happens? It is important to realise that everyone has the potential and ability to achieve great success. But unfortunately, most of them fail to identify their strengths. Our negative thoughts and faulty beliefs can hinder our progress, impacting our self-esteem, particularly those thoughts that we have developed due to our faulty childhood experiences.

This book encourages you to let go of past experiences, overcome your limiting beliefs, develop faith and belief in your ability to make it and take action to achieve your desires. Doing this will enable you to achieve your goals and attract success and happiness.

The book begins with a personal story followed by definitions and ranges of self-esteem, its components, and the importance of developing adequate self-esteem to enhance overall well-being and achieve dreams. From chapters on the formation and cycle of self-esteem, the reader will gain insight into how self-esteem is formed based on childhood experiences and keeps wavering based on their situations and experiences.

The book addresses the signs and symptoms of low self-esteem and its consequences on different aspects of their lives and provides practical tips and strategies to overcome low self-esteem. It encourages the reader to stop comparing or degrading themselves, recall past achievements, acknowledge their flaws and fears, take positive inputs, be surrounded by positive people, set realistic goals, celebrate their wins, learn something new, get into shape, and come out of their comfort zone to enhance their confidence and take actionable steps to achieve their goals.

To develop a growth mindset and foster positive thinking, readers are introduced to advanced techniques like cognitive restructuring, behavioural activation, positive self-talk, daily affirmations, gratitude journaling, gradual exposure therapy, mindfulness meditation, strengths identification, thought records, and visualisation and imagery.

The book also explores NLP (neuro-linguistic programming) techniques, helping the readers with the tools to reprogram their minds and behaviour to enhance their self-esteem, followed by positive affirmations and motivational quotes to enhance their confidence and overall development.

This book will help you become the architect of your destiny and convert your dreams into reality.

ABOUT THE AUTHOR

Shabnam Omer is a dedicated and dynamic professional. Counsellor, corporate trainer, emotional intelligence coach, and motivational speaker. Owing to her passion, she also has a YouTube channel, which goes by the name "The Counselling Corner." Armed with a passion for empowering people and a deep understanding of adult learning principles and human behaviour, Shabnam believes in connecting with people and helping them overcome their challenges and reach their highest potential by sharing real-time examples and her personal experiences.

She also takes up individual and group counselling sessions to help people resolve their issues and instil a ray of hope in their lives. She ensures all her sessions and workshops are dynamic, energetic, interactive, and result-oriented. She has a postgraduate degree in social work, specialising in medical and psychiatry, from PSG College of Arts and Science and has cleared UGC/NET, a PG Diploma in Counselling, an advanced diploma in HRM, an E-Master certification in business and communication skills, and a corporate trainer certification for IATD, Synergy.

She has an overall experience of 22+ years in psychological counselling, designing and conducting training sessions for students, teachers, and corporate employees.

She conducts training sessions on improving personal effectiveness, mental health, and well-being, stress and anger management, POSH Act, effective communication skills, problem-solving, self-esteem enhancement, time management, work-life balance, conflict resolution, and team-building skills for corporate clients and educational institutions. She also conducts sessions on exam stress and anxiety management, adaptive behaviour, effective study tips, sexuality and puberty, time management, and goal-setting workshops for students.

Her sessions have been a game-changer for numerous people from organisations. She specialises in creating engaging and interactive training sessions with many activities that address the specific needs of diverse people across various industries. Her biggest strength is that she explains the concepts by citing real-time examples and her personal experiences, making the attendees connect easily and adopt them in their lives to transform themselves.

Email: Shabnam.omer@thecounsellingcorner.co

Contact No.: 9986672470

YouTube: https://www.youtube.com/@thecounselingcorner

Facebook: https://www.facebook.com/TheCounsellingCorner.co

Instagram: https://www.instagram.com/thecounsellingcorner.co

linkedin:

https://www.linkedin.com/in/shabnam-khatija-omer

WHAT WILL YOU GAIN FROM READING THIS BOOK?

1. An understanding of self-esteem and its components.

2. An understanding of how self-esteem develops and keeps wavering based on past experiences and situations, especially childhood experiences.

3. Understand signs of low self-esteem and its negative impacts in various areas of life and take proactive steps to deal with it.

4. Identify your strengths and weaknesses, likes and dislikes, and skill sets, and set clear goals based on this knowledge.

5. The real-life stories and examples will motivate and inspire you to cope with challenges and be resilient.

6. Help you deal better with stress and anxiety, leading to better decision-making ability and enhancing your overall well-being.

7. You will learn and be able to apply practical tips and techniques to enhance the various components of self-esteem.

8. Various strategies to enhance your confidence, thereby enhancing your self-esteem and promoting your mental health.

9. How to enhance self-esteem using NLP techniques.

10. You will gain insight into the importance of positive affirmations in enhancing your confidence and positive thinking.

11. Will be able to take action and manifest your desires.

Chapter 1

INTRODUCTION

As a kid, I was a shy and introverted child. I was very thin; my family members, including my aunt and uncle, would tease me by calling me names, and I was always compared to my older sister, who was a very beautiful girl. This made me feel very low and unhappy, and it impacted my self-esteem drastically. I lived in a joint family in a huge bungalow consisting of 25 huge rooms, surrounded by 300 acres of coffee estate built by the East India Company. The house is boat-shaped and consists of many glass doors and windows.

As I was very shy, I was not comfortable facing people. So when I heard the vehicle sound, I understood that some visitors or guests had come. No matter what I was doing, I used to run and peep out through the window, and on seeing them, I used to run and hide, either in the washroom or into the coffee estate. I would desperately wait to hear the vehicle sound again to make sure the guest had left and come out of my hiding place.

Due to body shaming and constant comparison with my beautiful-looking sister, my self-esteem crashed. I still remember standing in front of the mirror and crying, asking God, "Why did he create me like this?" This impacted my academic performance to a great extent. I used to fail in three subjects and was put down by my teachers and teased by my classmates. Not only this, I was punished by my mother, who used to hit me with a stick and hurt me once by putting a hot spoon on my leg. I wasn't able to focus on my studies as most of the time; I was thinking and worrying about my looks. I was a very unhappy child and always felt that I didn't deserve love.

In primary school, I remained an extremely shy and withdrawn child and avoided participating in any extracurricular activities, such as theatre and dance, though I aspired to, due to fear and lack of confidence. Watching other students perform on stage, I felt very low and hoped God had blessed me, too, with those qualities and talents.

My situation became worse after an incident that took place when I was in 3rd grade. I aspired to learn dance, but my parents were not okay with enrolling me in the dance classes. My school organised a concert, and the students were preparing for a group dance performance. There was a requirement for one more girl for the group dance, so the dance teacher came up to my class and asked if anyone would volunteer to participate.

Though I had not practised and it was my first time, I gathered courage and volunteered to participate, and the teacher agreed. The teacher played the music and asked me to dance with the trained girls. I tried my level best by following them. Once the music stopped, everyone, including the teacher, laughed and made fun of me. This bitter experience hurt me to the extent that I decided I would never try dancing again in my life, and this damaged my self-esteem further. I continued being a sad and withdrawn child, hoping some miracle would happen and things would change for the better.

Things took a turn when I was promoted to 7th grade. My class teacher, who was also my history teacher, observed me closely and understood that I was disturbed about something. She took the time to speak to me in person and understand what was bothering me. Initially, I was reluctant to share, but I opened up to her regarding my concerns and my feelings.

The teacher held me tightly by my arms and said, "You have such lovely features; I am sure that you will grow into a beautiful lady." This made me feel so good—for the first time in my life, someone praised me. I accepted her appreciation, and every time I looked at myself in the mirror, I was reminded of her words. Instead of feeling bad about my lean body, I started focusing on my features and feeling good about myself. She told me one thing: I always tell my students who feel low when they are teased by others. She said, "Imagine yourself as the sun shining in the sky, and if the dogs look at you and bark, you should not pay attention; eventually, they will get tired and stop, and you will continue to shine, like the sun.".

I developed a strong liking for her. It is a known fact that if a student likes the teacher, then he or she will start liking his or her subject, too and will start performing well in it. The same thing happened to me, and I started focusing completely on learning history. When the test results were announced in the class, to my surprise, I realised that I had scored the highest in history compared to others in my class. Everyone in the class applauded me, making me feel very good about myself. The teacher then made me realise my potential to study well, saying when you can score so well in history, why not other subjects? This motivated me and enhanced my confidence. My liking towards her was so strong that I accepted everything she told me. I started putting my heart and soul into my studies. I got so busy with my studies that I completely stopped thinking and worrying about my looks. Gradually, I started improving my academic performance, passed all my subjects, and was appreciated by my father, the only person who showered love and appreciated me.

I continued to be a shy and withdrawn person and refrained from participating in any activities, and this pattern continued during my college days. The turning point in my life came again when I was pursuing my postgraduate degree in Masters of Social Work at PSG College of Arts and Science. An inter-college fest was organised, inviting participants from various reputed colleges. Suddenly, one of my professors walked into the class and announced the upcoming festival scheduled for next week. To my surprise, calling out my name, he declared that I would be representing my college and handed over the speech to me.

I was speechless, overwhelmed with tension. I gathered courage and said to him, " No, I won't be able to do it. I have never faced an audience; I suffer from stage fright. It would end up in a disaster. I pleaded with him, saying, "Please, could you consider someone better to do this task?"

However, he was very rigid. Ignoring my pleas, he left the class for the staffroom. I ran behind him, and with tears, I pleaded with him again and again. But in vain. The other professors who were observing this intervened, saying, "If she is not comfortable giving the speech, why are you insisting? Why don't you ask some other student to take it up?" But the professor wouldn't listen to anyone and responded firmly, stating, "I know she can do it, and she is going to do it. That's my final decision, and I don't wish to discuss this further."

I understood that there was no point pleading with the professor. I returned to the class and desperately pleaded with my classmates, asking if anyone could take up the responsibility in my place. Seeing me in tears, one student agreed but had no courage to speak to the professor. He said that he would do the speech if told by the professor. Unfortunately, the professor remained stern and was not ready to yield. Soon, I realised that I had no other option but to take up the responsibility of giving the speech.

Trust me, since then, I have been so anxious and had sleepless nights. My mind was preoccupied with all negative thoughts: What would happen if I stopped the speech midway or made a mistake? "People would laugh at me." My childhood memories, where everyone, including my teacher, laughed and made fun of me when I tried attempting to dance for the first time, came to my memory and made me feel more anxious. I was so anxious that I carried the speech paper everywhere I went and kept reading it again and again. Those few days before the speech were my toughest days.

On the day I had to deliver the speech, I was very scared and anxious. Standing behind the stage, I observed students from various colleges presenting their speeches one after another. I thought to myself, "Oh my God, they are speaking so well. What am I going to do?" Finally, when my college name was announced, fear gripped me, and my heart started beating very fast. I could hear everyone asking me to go ahead, but I was frozen.

Suddenly, I noticed the professor on the opposite side of the stage staring at me. I realised it was too late now; nothing could happen, and I had no other option but to gather my courage and deliver the speech. I walked towards the podium. I felt everyone staring at me, and I got more anxious. I closed my eyes for a second and whispered to myself, "God, please help me," and I began my speech. As I continued, there was profound silence, and I could hear only my voice, and I slowly gained confidence.

Finally, I concluded the speech and heard the people applauding and some whispering, "Hey, who is this girl?" I felt a sense of relief when I stepped off the stage and was greeted with appreciation by my professors and friends, who complimented me for my confidence and pleasant voice. My professor commented, "I knew she would do it, and she did it." I felt so good about myself. I had done something that I thought was impossible for me to do all my life. I couldn't believe what I was feeling.

It was that day I realised that God had gifted me with the strength of public speaking and that I could face an audience. This significant achievement of my journey enhanced my self-esteem to some extent. I thought to myself, 'If only this professor had entered my life earlier and I had discovered this capability, I wouldn't have missed out on numerous opportunities in my childhood, and I could have been a happier child.'

Similarly, I believe that everyone has hidden potential that needs to be identified and nurtured. In my case, it was the professor who recognised my strength and brought it to the forefront. However, this doesn't happen in every case. So, you must do some introspection, seek constructive feedback from others, and identify your strengths. Step out of your comfort zone to achieve your dreams.

Following this event, I made sure that I seized every opportunity I got to stand before an audience. I volunteered to conduct classes for my classmates. This gradually enhanced my confidence.

Another incident that transformed me from an introvert to an extrovert. This was during my second year of postgraduation. Six students had opted for the specialisation, "Medical and Psychiatry." We were placed in different settings in remote areas for fieldwork. I was placed alone in a leprosy centre, and it took two buses to reach there. There wasn't a single female staff, and I had to interact with the male staff and the patients, collect information, and prepare reports. I was not comfortable and decided to opt-out. I tried requesting the department head to either send another student along with me or change my organisation, but she wouldn't agree to it. I even told her that I would quit college, but somehow she convinced me, telling me that I am a strong girl and she was sure I would do well.

After a few visits, I gained confidence, started interacting with everyone, and started enjoying my work. On my 5th visit to the centre, the department head visited the centre and was very happy to see me comfortably interacting with all and appreciated me. This incident in my life helped me get comfortable talking to even strangers rather than shying off. I owe my sincere gratitude to my teacher and professors who helped me along my journey to overcome my low self-esteem and gain confidence.

Life is not always a bed of roses. I aspired to pursue my M.Phil. and PhD at NIMHANS, where I did my block placement, and aspired to pursue my counselling career. But God had different plans. Once I completed my postgraduate degree, I stayed in my hometown for a year and took up teaching, as I had lost my father by then, and my mother was not okay with me pursuing my higher studies. She had plans to get me married off. After a year, I got married into a conservative family, wherein I was not allowed to pursue my studies or career. But somehow, I convinced my father-in-law to complete my PG Diploma in Counselling and cleared my UGC/Net exam.

I had two lovely daughters, and I got busy taking care of my family, so I was happy. Suddenly, after 11 years of my happy married life, life took a turn. Something terrible happened, and I had no other option but to leave my house along with my two daughters, who were very small then. I was in severe depression and even tried ending my life twice, but I escaped. My self-esteem crashed. I felt my life had ended; I did not have the confidence. I thought, How am I going to survive?

I moved to my parent's house along with my two little daughters. Seeing my condition and fearing that I would try attempting such things again, my sister decided to get me to Bangalore and get me a job to divert my mind. Through her friend, she arranged for an interview in a reputed consultancy. All she told me was, "Go and meet my friend, and he will offer you a job." But, to my surprise, when I reached the consultancy, I had a proper interview. I couldn't answer any questions related to recruitment and staffing, which were different vertices of which I had no clue. I had transformed into a conservative housewife and had no clue as to how the outside world works.

Finally, after the interview, I was offered the post of a counsellor based on my qualifications and good communication skills but offered a very minimum salary to survive in a place like Bangalore. But I took it up as I was very sure I would not get a job elsewhere with the state I was in. I was very depressed, crying most of the time, with zero confidence.

For a week, everything seemed to be easy; all I had to do was interact with different teams and understand how they worked. Then, I was asked to meet and counsel the walk in candidates. It was in 2007, a recession time wherein many people lost their jobs and would walk in desperately looking for a job. Initially, I found it very difficult as I would be surrounded by many candidates, especially men who were desperate to meet me, hoping that I would help them find a job. Nearly 100 to 150 walk-ins per day. It was overwhelming, and many times, I used to get off my seat and run to the washroom and cry. I had sleepless nights and thought I would quit the job, but then I thought, "What would I do without the job? How am I going to pay the PG fees?" And I would return to the job the next morning.

I still remember that all I used to do was collect CVs from candidates and ask the question, "Tell me something about yourself." I wouldn't even listen to what they were saying. I would then tell them, "I will get back to you", and send them off.

As I was working, I used to get sudden flashbacks of the negative experiences I had, and tears would roll down in the presence of the candidates. One day, one of my colleagues noticed this; she held my hand and took me to the cafeteria for a coffee. She then told me, "It doesn't look good to cry before the candidates; you need to learn to control your emotions." She said one thing, which I still remember, and also told it to others. "Just forget the past and forgive the ones who have hurt you; God will take care of them." Just focus on your work and try to be happy." Her guidance changed my thought process, and I accepted her advice and started implementing it. I found relief and felt much better.

I put all my focus on my job. Started interacting with the people, trying to understand their concerns and needs, trying to connect with the recruiters, understanding their requirements, and trying to put the right candidates with the respected recruiters and assist them in getting placed. As I was interacting with people, I realised that I was in a much better position compared to many who were struggling. I came across women who were harassed by their spouses, physically abused, and had nowhere to go. They did not have any family support, unlike me. I got so busy counselling them and assisting them to get a job that in no time, I overcame my depression and was much more confident and happy. I realised the best way to overcome depression is to keep yourself busy. Another is to listen to others' pain and help people in need. By helping others, you get a lot of satisfaction and also tend to forget your pain and overcome your depression.

A few months passed, and my boss changed. My new boss, who was a very strict man, sat with me to understand what work I do. He then instructed me to maintain the details of the candidates in an Excel sheet and send weekly reports to him. I was shocked, as I did not even know how to turn on the computer. So how am I going to maintain the Excel sheets and send reports? It was overwhelming. I went up to my boss's cabin and told him directly that I would not be able to maintain Excel sheets and send him weekly reports as I didn't know how to operate the computer. He was shocked and shouted, saying, "Who the hell hired you for the job when you can't even operate the system?"

That night I couldn't sleep and kept thinking about what to do. I realised that I had only two options: one is to quit the job, and the second is to take someone's help, learn, and do the job. But if I opt for the first option, where would I go? The next morning I left the office half an hour early and requested the receptionist to help me turn on the system and teach me the basics. She was kind enough to help me. I started doing trial and error and trying to learn.

My seat was placed in the centre of two departments and close to the restroom. So every time someone passed by. I used to call them randomly and ask for their help. Within one month, I learned Excel as well as how to prepare reports and send them to my boss, who was surprised and appreciated me. This boosted my self-esteem to a great level. As people usually say, "Everything happens for good," I realised that nothing is impossible; if we are determined, focused, and put in hard work with confidence, we can turn the impossible into possible. Everything depends on our mindset, so adopt a never give up attitude and pursue your goals.

After a year and a half, I got another opportunity to learn. We were recruiting for Air India, approximately 700+ candidates. The person who was maintaining the MIS quit the job due to some emergency, and there was an immediate requirement for an MIS person to maintain the data. Suddenly I was called upon by the team leader, who told me that I would be handling the MIS. I wasn't confident and turned her down. She then said it was an order from my boss, who then convinced me by telling me that he was very confident that I would do a good job. I had no other option but to agree to it. Again, I started taking help from others and maintaining the MIS. Very soon I was able to grasp it and started enjoying the work. That month I received the best performance award for the month, and my confidence in my ability increased. I realised that everything seems to be difficult initially, but once we start doing it wholeheartedly, it becomes easy. So don't lose good opportunities assuming that you would not be able to do it; just go for it and put in hard work. You will surely succeed.

KEY TAKEAWAYS FROM CHAPTER 1

1. Identify your strengths and areas of concern by reflection. Make use of your strengths to grow and work on your areas of concern and convert them into strengths.

2. Believe in your abilities and adopt a never give up attitude.

3. Avoid comparing yourself with others or their performance, as this will kill your self-esteem. Instead, compare yourself with your previous achievements.

4. Face your fears with confidence and overcome them; otherwise, they will become the roadblocks for you to achieve your dreams. Overcoming fear will lead to personal and professional development.

5. Love and respect yourself and have confidence in your abilities to make it in life.

6. Don't let go of any opportunities due to self-doubt. Grab every opportunity that comes your way. Remember, good opportunities don't knock on your door again and again.

7. Learn to take calculated risks in life. Try out new things with confidence. If you fear taking risks, you will never try, and that will hinder your progress.

8. Get out of your comfort zone; only then will you get opportunities to grow and succeed in life.

9. Try to be surrounded by positive people who will inspire and motivate you and contribute to your success.

10. Seek mentors who will guide and inspire you to grow.

11. Avoid paying much attention to what others think and say about you. Remember, other people's opinions about you don't define your reality; you are what you think you are.

12. Learn to forget and forgive those who have wronged you, not for their sake but for your mental peace and happiness.

13. Keep yourself busy to avoid overthinking and worrying. Remember, helping others in need is one of the best

ways to overcome pain and depression and achieve happiness in life.

14. Changes and challenges are inevitable. We cannot avoid them. So accept life as it is and go with the flow. Remember, the more challenges you face, the stronger you will become.

15. Don't stop learning. Continue to broaden your knowledge by reading books, attending workshops, and listening to podcasts.

16. Strive hard to become the best version of yourself.

Chapter 2

UNDERSTANDING SELF-ESTEEM

"Believe you can, and you're halfway there."

– Theodore Roosevelt

Self-esteem is the overall evaluation of your self-worth or value. It involves your beliefs and feelings about your capabilities, competence, and the degree to which you feel worthy of love, respect, and success. Self-esteem is your attitude, perception, and beliefs about your abilities and limitations.

RANGES OF SELF-ESTEEM

The level of self-esteem isn't stable every time. You may experience different levels of self-esteem based on the situation or experience. If you perform well in life and people appreciate you, your self-esteem may go high, but the moment you meet with failure and face criticism from others, your self-esteem may go down. Let me explain this to you by citing a few real-life examples.

There was a very talented and passionate teacher in a school, and she used to teach biology to high school students. The children loved her a lot, and she received a lot of appreciation from their parents. Her self-esteem was high. During the appraisal, the principal told her she would be handling middle school students the next academic year. She raised a question as to why she was being demoted to middle school. She was told that her classes had been consistently observed through the camera and found to be very noisy and that she lacked the ability to manage the high school students.

Hearing this criticism, her self-esteem crashed, and she became withdrawn and stopped interacting with others. I observed her a couple of times and noticed that she seemed very lost and upset, and I, being a counsellor, tried talking to her. With eyes filled with tears, she said, "I am not a good teacher." She then narrated what happened and said, "I have resigned from my job and will never take up teaching again in my life."

I was shocked, as I had always received good feedback regarding her teaching, and she was my daughter's teacher, too. I told her, "That she is a good teacher, that children love her, and she should not quit teaching." But she was in so much distress and would not accept it. I then encouraged her to apply for a job at an international school and told her that if she wasn't interested, she didn't need to take up the offer but to attend the interview. My only intention was to alter her negative thinking and limiting beliefs, enhance her self-esteem, and make her feel confident.

Since I insisted, she applied for a job in an international school and within 10 days got a call for an interview. I pushed her to attend the interview, and she got the offer with a much better package, and her self-esteem improved. After serving the notice period of two months, she joined her new job. The next year she got nominated for the best teacher's award and became more confident.

This example clearly states how people's self-esteem varies based on their situations and experiences. So, you must strive to develop a self-esteem that will remain constant, irrespective of life experiences and situations. This will enable you to enhance your emotional and mental health status and lead a happy and stress-free life.

HIGH SELF-ESTEEM

People with high self-esteem believe in their self-worth and have a positive attitude towards themselves. They are aware of their strengths and weaknesses.

Individuals with high self-esteem generally

- possess a positive perception of themselves.

- Love and respect themselves.

- They trust, have confidence, and faith in their abilities.

- They are resilient and can bounce back from setbacks and challenges.

Raju, my maid's son, was from a poor family. He lost his father at the age of six and faced a lot of challenges in his life. He was raised by a single mother and understood her difficulties. When he was studying in 12th grade, he noticed the challenges his village was facing. His village lacked basic facilities like drinking water and medical facilities. He wanted to alter the situation in his village but felt helpless. He realised he needed to be in power to make a difference in his village. So he decided to become an IAS officer.

Though he was an average student in school and was discouraged by his teachers, he decided to pursue his dream. He started working hard, saved his pocket money, and bought general knowledge books. He was focused on his goal and avoided all distractions. He managed to score 88% in 12th grade and took up the arts stream in college.

He couldn't afford coaching classes. One of his professors became aware of his passion and offered to help him by providing the necessary materials. He started preparing day and night. After his graduation, he got a job offer in a private company, but he refused to accept it. Although he met with many challenges and setbacks, he wouldn't give up and was determined to achieve his goal. He failed in two attempts, but in the third attempt, he cleared the exam and made his mother and village proud.

Raju's success portrays his unwavering faith and confidence in himself, his determination to achieve his goal no matter what, consistent hard work, resilience, and perseverance. Nothing could stop him from achieving his goal.

MODERATE OR ADEQUATE SELF-ESTEEM

"Believe in yourself and all that you are. Know that there is something inside you that is greater than any obstacle."

– Christian D. Larson

People with moderate self-esteem generally

- Have a realistic and balanced perception of themselves.

- They can acknowledge their strengths and weaknesses.

- They can handle constructive criticism and setbacks without impacting their self-worth.

Let me explain this with an example.

Sherin belonged to a family of doctors, and her parents wanted her to become a heart surgeon. As a child, she was interested in taking up the medical profession, but when she reached 12th grade, she realised that she was not interested in the science stream and that her strength lay in writing, and she aspired to become a writer.

Although her parents were totally against her decision, she decided to pursue her dream of becoming a writer. She had a clear goal in mind of what she wanted to pursue.

Sherin faced criticism and objections from her parents and relatives, but she took it positively and was firm with her decision. Her moderate self-esteem helped her to deal with her setbacks and others' opinions in a positive manner, and she did not allow it to impact her self-worth. Despite all the challenges, she pursued her passion with determination, became a successful writer, and was very proud of her decision.

Today, her family is very proud of her. Her story illustrates the importance of having unwavering faith in one's abilities, acknowledging strengths and weaknesses, making a constructive decision, and being resilient in pursuing one's passion.

LOW SELF-ESTEEM

Individuals with low self-esteem

- Lack confidence in their abilities.

- Have a negative self-image.

- Don't love and respect themselves.

- Find it difficult to embrace appreciation and praise.

- Struggle with self-doubt and feel low and unmotivated.

- Unable to cope with the challenges and adversities.

Low self-esteem, if not addressed promptly, may lead to psychological issues like depression, anxiety, and eating disorders.

Let me explain this by citing a real-time example of a child who was referred to me for counselling.

Simi, a 10th-grade student, was from a well-off family. She was disturbed as her family compared her with her sister, who was an all-rounder, scoring high in academics and winning many awards in sports. The comments from her grandparents and her mother made her feel very low and killed her self-esteem. She began to believe that she was not good enough and did not deserve love from anyone.

She was constantly overthinking and worrying, and this affected her academic performance drastically. Being in 10th grade, she had constant pressure to perform well, and this worsened her situation. This showed up in her behaviour. She became very sarcastic and started reacting to every small thing. She was always put down and laughed at in school. Her friends started disliking and avoiding her. She did not get the support of her teachers, had no one to vent her feelings, and got into depression.

Things became worse for Simi, and she started harming herself by cutting her hands with a blade, and it was terrible. As days went by, her condition worsened, and she got into severe depression, developed suicidal tendencies, and tried to jump from the 14th floor of her apartment. Her feelings got so overwhelmed that she also tried to strangle her sister.

Her parents took her for counselling, and she was also referred for psychiatric help. With the support of a counsellor, Simi learned that internal beauty is more important than her external appearance. She started feeling positive and got herself busy doing things she enjoyed, like painting and dancing. Simi scored high grades in her 12th grade. Now, she's in college studying engineering and doing well. Simi's story shows that with help, gaining confidence in one's ability, and accepting who you are, it is possible to overcome difficult times and perform well in life.

From Simi's example, you must have gained a clear understanding that faulty childhood experiences or childhood trauma like physical and verbal abuse and comparison can contribute to low self-esteem. It is possible to improve your self-esteem by gaining insight into your thoughts and emotions and seeking professional help.

Self-esteem varies across different areas of life—like academics, social interactions, and physical well-being. Some might feel great about their professional achievements but face challenges with low self-esteem in their relationships or personal lives. It's crucial to cultivate a consistent and healthy self-esteem that holds steady, regardless of the circumstances in any aspect of life.

COMPONENTS OF SELF-ESTEEM

To develop adequate self-esteem, it becomes crucial for you to focus on and develop the following components of self-esteem.

SELF-WORTH

"You alone are enough. You have nothing to prove to anybody."

– **Dr. Maya Angelou**

Self-worth is the value and importance you give to your life and achievements. It is an internal sense of being good enough and worthy of love and respect from others. It is a feeling that you possess good qualities and have achieved great things in life. It includes a sense of security and resilience.

My neighbour Renuka is an engineer and a passionate singer. She enjoyed expressing herself through her music. Her family did not appreciate this, but she knew her own worth. She did not pay attention to others' opinions regarding her passion for singing. Though her family was against her singing, she continued singing, embracing her self-worth. She was not dependent on external validation to follow her passion.

SELF-CONFIDENCE

"Confidence comes not from always being right but from not fearing to be wrong."

– Peter T. McIntyre."

Self-confidence means believing in yourself and trusting your abilities and what you can do. It is having a positive attitude about yourself. Confident people don't doubt their ability. They are very assertive and positive and can set realistic and achievable goals and achieve them.

Aisha belonged to a conservative family and aspired to become a college professor, but her parents forced her into marriage. She had two sons and got busy taking care of her family. When her sons started going to school, she decided to pursue her passion. She started preparing for the UGC/NET exam, a qualification for professors, with the help of a professor. Within four months, she managed to collect all the study material, worked day and night, and cleared her exam successfully on her first attempt, surprising her family and friends, and got an appointment in a reputed college as a professor. Aisha's willpower, determination, and confidence in her abilities helped her to achieve her dreams.

SELF-RESPECT

"Respect yourself if you would have others respect you."

– Baltasar Gracián

Self-respect means understanding your worth and treating yourself with compassion and dignity. It is loving, respecting, and accepting yourself for who you are, with your flaws and strengths. It is the basis of any healthy relationship. Only if you love and respect yourself will others love and respect you. So, learn to value yourself.

Shruti, a housewife, lived in a joint family with her in-laws. She was very committed to her family and, at the same time, never allowed anyone to take advantage of or mistreat her. She was very assertive while communicating with her family and politely refused to do anything she wasn't comfortable with. She expressed her feelings and views openly and always stood up for herself. She knew her worth and treated herself with honour.

SELF-IMAGE

"The way you think about yourself determines your reality."

– Geneen Roth

Self-image reflects your thoughts, feelings, and views about yourself. It's a picture you tend to form in your mind about how you look, your ability to do things, and how you assume others perceive you. People with low self-image lack confidence and have low self-esteem.

Example:

My friend's daughter, Sheela, views herself as a caring and friendly person. She believes that she is very good at academics and sports and is always ready to help others in need. All her classmates loved her for her caring and helpful nature and saw her as an intelligent and kind-hearted person. She received a lot of appreciation from her teachers. This positive self-image helped Sheela to be more positive and assertive and overcome any challenges she faced with confidence.

SELF-EFFICACY

Self-efficacy means believing in your ability to do things or complete tasks successfully. It's feeling confident about your ability to overcome all your challenges and achieve your desired goals.

Example:

A person may accept an offer to address a huge crowd for the first time as he or she has the confidence that they can do it by preparing for the speech and practising.

*"To succeed, people need a sense of self-efficacy,
to struggle together with resilience to meet the inevitable
obstacles and inequities of life."*

– Albert Bandura

An IT professional with two years of work experience had to do a difficult coding task that he had never done earlier. Despite the challenge, Robert believed in his skills and ability to learn and perform. He thinks, "I might not know it now, but I can learn and figure it out." This belief in his ability to learn and solve problems is Robert's self-efficacy he possesses. It helps him approach new challenges with confidence, believing that he will succeed no matter how tough the task is.

SELF-PERCEPTION

Self-perception is how you view and perceive yourself. Like what kind of person you think you are. It's like forming opinions about yourself based on your previous experiences. A picture you have of yourself, including your physical, mental, and social characteristics—your body image is an example of self-perception.

> *"When you know yourself, you are empowered.*
> *When you accept yourself, you are invincible."*

> **– Tina Lifford**

A social worker working in a child welfare department perceives himself to be a very efficient and committed worker. He is a kind-hearted and service-oriented person, and he sees himself as a very caring and helpful person, as he enjoys helping others, especially the children, and feels very satisfied when he makes a difference in their lives. This image that he has formed about himself as a caring and helpful person is his self-perception. This self-perception guides his actions in different scenarios, reinforcing the image he has created about himself.

SELF-COMPASSION

> *"You've been criticising yourself for years, and it hasn't worked.*
> *Try approving of yourself and see what happens."*

> **– Louise L. Hay**

"Self-compassion is key because when we're able to be gentle with ourselves in shame, we're more likely to reach out, connect, and experience empathy."

– Brené Brown

Self-compassion is being kind and understanding towards yourself when you are undergoing some pain or challenges. When you make some mistakes or meet with failures, you treat yourself the same way you would treat your friend in a similar situation. It is gaining insight into how everyone makes mistakes and how it's okay to make mistakes. It is important to learn from our mistakes and never repeat them. It helps one to prioritise their well-being and become resilient. It involves three components: self-kindness, common humanity, and mindfulness.

SELF-ACCEPTANCE

"To be yourself in a world that is constantly trying to make you something else is the greatest accomplishment."

– Ralph Waldo Emerson

Self-acceptance is accepting yourself the way you are with your strengths and limitations without judging. It is accepting your imperfections. You feel comfortable being your authentic self.

It is an ability to accept yourself completely without any changes or expectations. It is demonstrated through unconditional positive regard for oneself.

Rajesh, an accountant working for a multinational company, stammers a lot while speaking. He is overweight and short and is suffering from hormonal imbalance issues. Sometimes, people do advise him to reduce his weight. But instead of feeling bad or inferior, he accepts himself as he is and is very cheerful and confident about himself. He does not worry about what others might think or say about him. He firmly believes that "others' opinions about him do not define his reality" and is happy the way he is.

SOCIAL COMPETENCE

Being socially competent means having the ability to form deep connections, communicate effectively with empathy, be assertive, and listen attentively to others, considering their viewpoints and making them feel heard, respected, and valued. This enables us to foster a healthy and meaningful connection with others both in personal and professional life. It's having the ability to communicate effectively, work in cooperation with others, and build and maintain a long-lasting relationship with others. It will enable one to turn the casual acquaintance into a deeper connection. People with high social competence are admired by many. An effective leader requires this trait.

My niece possesses exceptional interpersonal skills and is admired by everyone in her college. She is capable of influencing people easily by communicating warmth and understanding. She listens to people when they talk by paying close attention, focusing on non-verbal cues, reading between the lines, understanding their perspectives and unsaid feelings, and responding accordingly. As she can gauge people's emotions and respond empathetically, she can make meaningful connections in life. She can easily connect and communicate with people of all age groups, speaking to them with great respect.

AUTONOMY

"The greatest gift you can give yourself is the freedom to be who you truly are, aligned with your values and dreams."

– Steve Maraboli

Autonomy means you are given the freedom and independence to make your own choices and decisions in life, keeping in mind your values and goals rather than following what others ask or want you to do. It is about being independent. If you have the freedom to make independent decisions, you will be motivated to set realistic goals that align with your values, work consistently towards them, and achieve great success in life.

Ayesha, a 12th-grade student, a multi-talented girl, was the topper in the class. Her parents aspired to make her a doctor. But she wasn't interested in the medical profession. Keeping in mind her mental health and happiness, Ayesha's parents gave her the freedom to choose her career. Ayesha explored different options and decided to enrol in the commerce stream. She aspired to become an event manager for a multinational company. Ayesha had the autonomy and freedom to decide for herself and make her own choices.

RESILIENCE

"The greatest glory in living lies not in never falling, but in rising every time we fall."

– Nelson Mandela

A resilient person can deal with the challenges and setbacks in life with confidence, bounce back successfully, and start all over again. Resilience is accepting life as it is, becoming emotionally and mentally strong, and moving ahead despite all the challenges and hardships you encounter. Resilient people are happier and more successful in life. The more challenges they face, the stronger they become.

Let me share my example.

Suddenly, I was diagnosed with third-stage cancer and had to undergo major surgery followed by six cycles of chemotherapy. I had to take a break from the school where I was associated as a counsellor. After my last cycle of chemotherapy, I decided to resume my work. I discussed this with one of my friends, who demotivated me, telling me that there was a possibility that the children would not accept me as I had lost my hair. This impacted my self-esteem, and I decided to stay back at home. But my children, who are my strong pillars of strength, suggested I give it a try and then take the final call.

To my surprise, when I visited several classes on my first day back to school, the children and the staff welcomed me, conveying that they were anticipating my return and were praying for my speedy recovery. Teachers were happy and said that I was a great source of inspiration for them and that they wanted me to work the same way as I did earlier. My example clearly shows that allowing other people's negative opinions to impact us will lower our confidence and prevent us from moving ahead in life. If we are resilient and determined, have confidence in our abilities, and have the support of others, we can overcome our challenges and emerge successfully.

All the above components of self-esteem are interrelated. You should try developing every component to enhance your self-esteem and achieve success in life. For example, positive self-worth and self-image will enhance your confidence and vice versa. Develop a positive mindset and a never give up attitude. Remember, nothing is impossible in life. So remove the word "impossible" from your life's dictionary.

KEY TAKEAWAYS OF CHAPTER 2

1. Self-esteem is an individual's overall evaluation of his or her self-worth or value.

2. Self-esteem is not stable and keeps varying based on one's situation or experience.

3. High self-esteem is related to a sense of self-worth and a positive attitude towards oneself.

4. Moderate self-esteem is associated with having a realistic and balanced perception, acknowledging one's strengths and weaknesses, and having the ability to handle constructive criticism and setbacks.

5. Low self-esteem involves a lack of confidence, having a negative self-image, a lack of love and respect for oneself, finding it difficult to accept appreciation and rewards, and struggling with self-doubt.

6. Key components of self-esteem:

    Self-worth: value and importance you give to your life and achievements.

Self-confidence: belief in your abilities to overcome the challenges and adversities of life.

Self-Respect: Understanding your worth and treating yourself with compassion and dignity.

Self-Image: Self-image reflects your thoughts, feelings, and views about yourself.

Self-Efficacy: Belief in your ability to do things or complete tasks successfully.

Self-Perception: Self-perception is how you view and perceive yourself based on your thoughts and experiences.

Self-compassion: being kind and understanding towards yourself when you are undergoing some pain or challenges.

Self-acceptance: Self-acceptance is accepting yourself the way you are, with your strengths and limitations, without judging.

Social Competence: having the ability to form deep connections, communicate effectively with empathy, be assertive, and listen attentively to others, considering their viewpoints and making them feel heard, respected, and valued.

Autonomy: having the freedom and independence to make your own choices and decisions in life, keeping in mind your values and goals rather than following what others ask or want you to do.

Resilience: Having the ability to deal with the challenges and setbacks in life with confidence, bounce back successfully, and start all over again.

7. Interconnected Nature:

Components of self-esteem are interconnected and can influence each other positively or negatively. Developing healthy self-esteem involves cultivating each component and addressing negative thought patterns.

Chapter 3

FORMATION OF SELF-ESTEEM

"Self-esteem is not dependent on external compliments
and appreciation, but rather through self-introspection,
facing and overcoming challenges and adversities,
and adopting a never-to-give-up attitude."

– Anonymous.

Growing up starts in infancy and continues as a child. Your self-esteem depends on how your family and friends treated you as a child. Your self-esteem will drop if you have experienced rejection, been jeered at, criticised, neglected, or unnecessarily blamed. Conversely, if you were accepted, praised, and shown warmth and affectionate love in addition to feeling secure, then your self-esteem would be fair.

As teenagers, you may find yourself comparing your looks with others, academic performance, or social status. This may make you feel low about yourself, wanting to be like others around you; this could negatively impact your self-esteem. Confidence can also be built through performing well in academics or sports where teachers, parents, and other students become appreciative and complimentary of it; thus, getting positive feedback from other people can bring about confidence, which would result in better academic performance.

As adults, how you perform at work, establish and maintain relationships with others, and achieve your achievements will impact your emotions and how you perceive yourself. If you receive appreciation for your performance from your boss, positive feedback for your speech, or a compliment from your friend regarding your outfit, you will feel confident, and your self-esteem will be high. But if you are constantly criticised for your work or scolded for submitting the project late or reporting late to the office, you will feel bad, and your confidence will drop.

The perception you have about yourself also matters. If you think positively and have a positive attitude about yourself, feel you deserve love and respect, and have confidence in your abilities to make and face the challenges life throws and emerge successfully, your self-esteem will increase automatically. Remember, you should first love and respect yourself; only then will others love and respect you.

To build adequate self-esteem, you need to do self-introspection, gain self-awareness, and accept that you are struggling with low self-esteem. Only if you accept will you be able to take appropriate steps to overcome it. Identify your negative thinking patterns and try replacing them with positive ones; overcome your limiting beliefs; understand your strengths and areas of concern. Based on your strengths and skill sets, set realistic and achievable goals and start working consistently towards achieving them. Be cheerful and passionate, and establish and maintain a healthy and long-lasting relationship with others by improving your conversation skills and being empathetic.

Let go of negative habits that don't benefit you, and try developing good habits, like reading, consuming positive content, waking up early, exercising regularly, and eating a balanced diet. Try looking at the positive in every situation, no matter how challenging they are, and have a positive attitude towards yourself and others. The most crucial thing to enhance your self-esteem is to love and respect yourself and have confidence in your abilities; nothing can stop you from achieving your dream.

Example

Nisha, my friend's daughter, was from a wealthy family. She received a lot of love and affection from her parents. She was multi-talented, good in academics and extracurricular activities, and got appreciation from teachers and her parents. She was fair and slim and received compliments from friends and relatives. Her parents were always there when she was in need. She grew up as a cheerful and confident girl. She was happy from within, and this was reflected in her behaviour; she was very kind and helpful to others and was loved and appreciated by all. This made her feel great, and she developed a positive attitude about herself.

On the other hand, her brother Salim was very naughty, and their parents received constant complaints from the school. He was not interested in studies and scored very low in academics. He was very aggressive and often picked fights with other children. Their parents were fed up with the complaints, treated him harshly, and kept putting him down, assuming that if shamed, he would change for the better. He was always compared to his sister, Nisha, who was good in academics and behaved well. This made Salim feel even worse, and his self-esteem was negatively impacted.

Nisha grew up with adequate self-esteem, as she had positive childhood experiences. Though she faced some challenges in college, like coping with peer pressure, she was able to overcome them and emerge successfully. But her brother, Salim, grew up with low self-esteem. He firmly believed that no one loved him and that he did not deserve love and respect. He developed a negative attitude about himself and others. He was rude and sarcastic with others, and people moved away from him. He had very few friends and, most of the time, felt lonely. He would not get along with his parents and was confined to the room most of the time.

As the days passed, he started consuming alcohol as a way of coping with his emotional distress and was admitted to the addiction centre to overcome his addiction problem. He was then referred to counselling and underwent therapy for nearly one year. The counsellor helped him gain self-awareness, overcome his low self-esteem, and build confidence. He then re-enrolled in college and graduated. Now, he is pursuing an MBA at a reputable college.

From Nisha's and Salim's examples, you must have understood the role of childhood experiences, positive or negative, in shaping a person's self-esteem. If you had a happy childhood experience with people around to care for and love you and received appreciation and praise, you will have adequate self-esteem. But if you had negative experiences like neglect, rejection, and criticism, your self-esteem would be inadequate. But nothing to worry about. The good news is that your self-esteem can be enhanced by working consistently and taking professional help if required.

THE CYCLE OF SELF-ESTEEM

The range of self-esteem keeps changing based on the situation or experiences. When things are going well, like when you perform well in school or at work, win a competition, receive appreciation for a dish you prepared, or get a promotion, then your self-esteem will be adequate. You will feel happier and more energetic, be able to focus on your work better and start attracting more positivity and success in life.

On the other hand, if you don't get attention and appreciation, meet with repeated failures, or face criticism, the range of your self-esteem may drop. You might feel low and unmotivated, your confidence might drop down, your focus and concentration will be low, and you might lose interest in your studies or work. This may lead to further distress and failure in life. As you start experiencing negative feelings, you will attract more negativity in life.

To end this repeated cycle, you need to work hard consistently and take the help of a trusted and experienced person to overcome these challenges and develop an adequate and stable self-esteem that does not waver, no matter what challenges you encounter. You need to have a positive attitude, develop positive habits, and find alternative ways to enhance your self-esteem by identifying your strengths and working on your areas of concern.

SELF-ESTEEM AND CONFIDENCE

Self-esteem and confidence are closely related. If you love and respect yourself and trust your abilities to make it in life, your self-esteem will automatically go up. But with low confidence, negative self-thought, and self-doubt, your self-esteem will go down. So if you have trust in your abilities and the confidence to perform well, love and respect yourself, accepting the way you are, you will be able to set realistic and achievable goals, work towards them confidently, bounce back from setbacks, and this will promote your overall well-being, contributing to your personal and professional development.

On the other hand, when you start achieving your goals, performing well, and receiving praise and appreciation from others, your confidence level will go up, and as your confidence grows, your self-esteem will shoot up.

For example, if you possess the qualities and skills required for a good counsellor and have successfully helped people in need resolve their issues, it can make you feel confident in helping others. Then, as you successfully help more and more people, your confidence grows, enhancing your self-esteem to a greater level. It's like a vicious circle where having adequate self-esteem and being confident go together to make you stronger and happier.

WHY SHOULD ONE HAVE ADEQUATE SELF-ESTEEM?

Importance of self-esteem

Self-esteem plays a vital role in one's personal and professional development. It helps promote emotional, mental, and social health. It helps an individual to make rational decisions, resolve problems, and set and achieve realistic goals with confidence and perseverance.

1. Adequate self-esteem promotes the mental health of the person, while low self-esteem is directly linked to mental health issues like depression and anxiety disorders.

2. People with adequate self-esteem view failures and setbacks as opportunities to learn and grow. They have a never give up attitude and keep trying until they succeed. They can cope with

challenges and stressful situations, are emotionally balanced, and bounce back from setbacks.

3. They can establish and maintain healthy and long-lasting relationships with others. Their emotional intelligence is high; they can recognise and manage their emotions, as well as understand others' feelings and respond appropriately. As they communicate effectively with empathy and assertiveness, they can influence people and establish a deeper connection. They also set clear boundaries and enforce them consistently.

4. They are resilient, as adequate self-esteem means they do not stay hooked on what does not go well; instead, they take it as an opportunity to learn and become stronger. They view failures as a part of their journey towards success. This enhances their ability to recover from challenges more swiftly and at a better pace, keeping themselves optimistic.

5. Those with healthy self-esteem can establish smarter goals and persistently endeavour to meet them. SMART goals: Specific, Measurable, Achievable, Reliable, and Time-bound with evaluation of progress or adjustments & rewards. Belief in their ability to achieve is the inner motivation that drives them consistently; great achievements are made leading up to great success in life.

6. Research shows that people with adequate or high self-esteem can manifest their desires and financial and health goals, succeed in their careers, and promote their overall well-being as they are proactive and take action. Adequate self-esteem leads to an increase in motivation level, enhances confidence, fosters positive thinking, and assists people in taking control of their lives, resulting in success in their careers.

7. We are all aware that change is inevitable. No one can resist change, and if we attempt, we will end up disappointed. We have no other option but to embrace change as a part of our journey and move ahead. Optimistic people consider change a part of their lives and take it as an opportunity to learn and grow. This helps them to advance in their life with confidence and hope. People with adequate self-esteem can gauge what is in their control and what isn't. Instead of trying to control things that are not in control, they focus on things under their control to achieve their desires.

8. People with adequate self-esteem are very innovative and creative. They strive to gain more and more knowledge and are ready to take risks and explore new and innovative things. They are adventurous and keep exploring new things. Their confidence in themselves enables them to come out of their comfort zone and explore new things without fear of failure. They possess a growth mindset, which helps them meet and face challenges with optimism and courage, as they view them as opportunities to grow rather than obstacles.

9. These people are open to change and consider others' views and perspectives; this enhances their ability to make rational and productive decisions in both their personal and professional lives. On the other hand, their confidence in their abilities helps them make independent decisions when required, and they don't depend on others for every small decision. People who lack confidence depend on others for every small decision due to fear of making the wrong decision as they lack trust in their abilities.

10. People with high or adequate self-esteem have a positive body image. They are happy and accept themselves the way they

look. They don't compare themselves with others and feel low. They are authentic and don't attempt to imitate and be like others. They accept themselves as they are with their strengths and shortcomings. While people with inadequate self-esteem keep comparing themselves with others, aspire to be like others, and feel low and depressed. One should understand that internal beauty is important and not the external appearance, as external beauty will fade away as they grow old. So, focus on what your body can do rather than how it looks.

TAKEAWAYS OF CHAPTER 3

1. Self-esteem is formed during childhood and is influenced by parents, friends, relatives, teachers, and peers.

2. As teenagers, your self-esteem may drop as you might compare yourself with others and their performance.

3. As adults, your work experiences, the quality of your relationships, and personal achievements or failures can impact your self-esteem.

4. A positive and growth mindset, self-awareness, a positive attitude, belief, and confidence in your abilities can go a long way in enabling you to develop adequate self-esteem that is stable.

5. The self-esteem cycle isn't stable and keeps changing based on positive and negative experiences.

6. Positive experiences like appreciation, achievements, and success enhance self-esteem, while negative experiences like rejection, failure, and criticism lower it.

7. Consistent effort is required to break the cycle and develop adequate self-esteem that does not waver based on experiences or situations.

8. Self-esteem and confidence are interdependent and go hand in hand.

9. Positive self-esteem forms the base for the confidence to pursue and achieve great things.

10. Success, achievements, and confidence in one's ability enhance self-esteem.

11. Adequate self-esteem and confidence are vital in enhancing emotional and mental health, and low self-esteem leads to psychological issues like depression, anxiety, and eating disorders.

12. Adequate self-esteem aids in recognising strengths and areas of concern, setting realistic and achievable goals, and pursuing them consistently to achieve desired outcomes.

13. It enhances motivation, fosters positive thinking and a positive attitude, promotes innovation and creativity, assists in making rational decisions, and contributes to personal and professional success.

14. It helps one accept and adapt to changes easily as part and parcel of life and try out new things by taking risks, leading to innovation and growth.

15. It instils a positive body image by helping people gain insight into their uniqueness and embrace their looks, understanding that what matters is how the body functions rather than how it looks, and leading a happy and fulfilling life.

Chapter 4

LOW SELF-ESTEEM

*"Low self-esteem is like driving through life
with your handbrake on."*

– Maxwell Maltz.

Low self-esteem means you think that you don't deserve love, appreciation, rewards, success, or positive attention. It involves constantly thinking negatively about yourself, leading to less confidence and self-assurance. People with low self-esteem often suffer from self-doubt, avoid new challenges, and pay a lot of attention to what others may think or say about them, which can become a roadblock for them to achieve success in their personal and professional lives.

CAUSES OF LOW SELF-ESTEEM

Various factors can trigger low self-esteem, and it usually comes from a mix of internal and external things.

Let's look at a few common causes as to why some people struggle with low self-esteem:

1. NEGATIVE CHILDHOOD EXPERIENCES

Negative childhood experiences are the main contributing factor to low self-esteem. Persistent criticism, rejection, or neglect during childhood can make you believe you're not worthy or good enough. If you've experienced trauma like physical, verbal, or sexual abuse, it can make you feel deeply ashamed and diminish your self-worth. These negative experiences in childhood can have an impact on how you view yourself, affecting how you relate to others and how you feel about yourself as you get older. Overcoming these feelings often involves talking to someone you trust, be it your family member or a friend, even a counsellor, and working consistently on building a more positive view of yourself.

Example

I know a girl named Amala who was studying in 8th grade. She lived in a joint family. She went through a tough time when her cousin' brother started sexually abusing her. When her parents found out, instead of helping her, they got upset with her and avoided her, blaming her for what had happened. Amala started believing that it was her fault and began to dislike herself a lot. At home, her family argued a lot about money problems, making things even harder for her. With all these difficulties, Amala found it tough to concentrate on her studies, and she didn't do well in her exams. Sadly, she even faced physical and verbal mistreatment because of her low scores. These negative experiences contributed to her low self-esteem.

Sharmila, the daughter of a single parent, stayed in her uncle's place as a child due to her education, as her mother was working in Delhi. She was not treated well by her aunt, who always put her down, calling her a dumb girl, and insulted her, telling her that her mother could not afford to buy expensive things. Due to persistent negative comments and criticism, Sharmila's self-esteem crashed. As a teenager, she grew up as an unhappy child, always comparing herself with her peers based on her appearance and status. Most of the time, she was found complaining, cribbing, and picking fights with her classmates. As a result, she was disliked by all her classmates, making her situation worse.

2. SOCIAL COMPARISONS

When you keep comparing yourself against others, it can make you feel like you're not as good as them, leading to low self-esteem. If you keep thinking about what others possess or how they look, you might feel like you're not as lucky as them. This will kill your self-confidence and make you unhappy about yourself.

Example:

My friend's daughter, Shruti, firmly believed she was not good-looking as she had a dark complexion, was short, and did not stand out much. She always looked at Eva, her classmate, who was very beautiful and had many talents. Shruti aspired to be like Eva and always felt low. Because of these feelings, Shruti wasn't happy about herself; she was always disturbed, and this directly impacted her behaviour; it made her act rude and sarcastic to others. As a result, her classmates avoided her, and she felt very lonely, assuming nobody loved her. All these issues took a toll on Shruti's emotional and mental health, and she went down drastically in her academic performance.

3. EXPOSURE TO SOCIAL MEDIA LEADING TO FALSE EXPECTATIONS

By viewing pictures in magazines or posts and videos on social media displaying others as perfect or successful in life, you may start comparing your looks or achievements and start feeling that you are not good enough.

For example, Radha, a stout and short girl, feels very low and upset when she sees pictures of models on social media, as she aspires to be slim and tall like them. Rajesh watches action movies and aspires to have a muscular body and perform actions like a hero. Thus, people develop false expectations by viewing unrealistic things on social media and aspiring to be like them, leading to disappointment and low confidence. People post their pictures on social media expecting likes and comments, and when they fail to get them, their self-esteem goes down.

My colleague's daughter struggled with low self-esteem as she always compared herself to her schoolmate, who was very popular on social media and had many friends. So she started accepting friend requests from unknown people and sending requests to strangers, and when she couldn't meet her expectations, her confidence went down drastically. You should avoid depending on social media to feel good about yourself.

4. EDUCATIONAL AND CAREER CHALLENGES

If you face constant problems in your school or work, such as putting in several hours of hard work but scoring fewer marks, or giving 100 percent and not getting recognition for your work, or receiving repeated criticism from your boss, or failing to crack the interview despite practising a couple of times, you will tend to lose your confidence and trust in your abilities, leading to low self-esteem.

After his MBA postgraduate degree, though Raj scored high academic grades, he faced multiple rejections in interviews due to poor communication skills. His confidence was impacted to the extent that he stopped attending interviews and decided to become an auto driver.

5. CHILDHOOD TRAUMA OR ABUSE

A person who has encountered any form of childhood trauma, be it physical, mental, or sexual abuse, may struggle with negative emotions like fear, anxiety, and sadness. This, in turn, may lead to self-criticism or a negative perception of oneself.

During her childhood, Katherine was physically and verbally abused by her stepmother, who made her perform all the household chores and compared her to her stepsister. This made her feel very inferior and impacted her self-worth.

Joseph, one of my clients, struggled with dyslexia, a reading disorder. Despite putting in hard work for hours together, he scored low in his academics. His father abused him physically for not performing well in academics and blamed his mother for his poor performance. This led to constant fights and arguments, and his parents separated. Joseph started blaming himself for his parents' conflicts and the separation and struggled with guilt feelings. These negative experiences made Joseph feel unworthy and dislike himself.

6. SEEKING PERFECTIONISM

"Perfectionism is the greatest enemy of progress;
by embracing the beauty of imperfection, you can allow it to be
your guide towards progress."

– Unknown

Perfectionism means you desire to be perfect in everything you do. There is nothing called perfectionism; it's just an illusion. Seeking perfection can lead to a lot of stress and anxiety, impacting your mental well-being and productivity.

Stephan, an architect from Calcutta, always aspired to be perfect in everything he did. Unfortunately, his desire to be perfect led to stress and anxiety, drastically impacting his mental health. He began to criticise himself and was very unhappy with his performance. He lost confidence and developed self-doubt, leading to low self-esteem. Setting unrealistic standards for yourself and expecting to be perfect in everything will lead to self-criticism and dissatisfaction and eventually kill your self-esteem. So embrace your imperfection and understand it's "ok" to be imperfect. Remember, we are all humans and grow by making mistakes and learning.

7. NEGATIVE SELF-TALK

"Don't let the noise of others drown out your inner voice,
And most importantly, dare to follow your heart.
and intuition."

– Steve Jobs

Negative self-talk is the inner voice talking to yourself. You have thousands of thoughts per day, and most of it is self-talk. When you constantly think and speak negatively about yourself, you tend to lose confidence and doubt your abilities. You will start focusing more on your problems and failures than your achievements, and this will impact the way you perceive yourself. Your self-talk is directly linked to your thoughts. If you think positively, your self-talk will be positive, and if you think negatively, it will be negative. Negative self-talk will demotivate you and stop you from taking action, thus hindering your progress. It will also impact your mental health. So, you need to keep track of your thoughts and self-talk and deliberately change the negative self-talk to a positive one.

EXAMPLES OF NEGATIVE SELF-TALK

- "I have always messed things up; I can't do anything right."

- "Nobody loves me; I'm so hopeless."

- "I'm not intelligent enough to grasp this; I'll never understand it."

- "I'm such a failure in life; I can't achieve success."

- "I look so ugly; I'm so short and stout."

- "I am not as good as others; I'm just useless."

- "I don't deserve love and respect; I always hurt others' feelings."

- "I'll never come up in life; I don't possess the ability."

- 'Everyone is avoiding me; I am not a good person.'

Maintain track of your negative self-talk and deliberately try to change it to positive.

EXAMPLES OF POSITIVE SELF-TALK

- "I may not know everything, but I can learn and understand things."

- "I've achieved some targets, and I'm capable of achieving more and more targets."

- "I may not feel great today, but I have unique qualities that make people admire me."

- "I'm blessed with unique talents and strengths that set me apart from others."

- "I possess the potential to achieve great success, and I'm constantly striving towards growth."

- "I'm blessed with the ability to cope with the challenges;"

- "I have qualities to influence people; I spread positivity to those around me."

- "I am not defined by what others think and say about me; I am what I think I am."

- "I inspire and motivate everyone; I am loved and appreciated by all."

8. HEALTH STATUS

Health issues, whether physical or mental, will impact performance and productivity, leading to frustration and self-doubt. Some physical health conditions can make one feel conscious about their looks, impacting their self-image. Mental health issues like anxiety disorders or depression can lead to persistent negative thinking and a lack of confidence. Health issues may also lead to social isolation and depression.

My friend, Radha, was beautiful and admired by everyone during her youth. She was diagnosed with breast cancer when she was 40 and underwent major surgery and six cycles of chemotherapy and radiation. This resulted in severe hair loss and changed her looks. She became conscious of her looks and avoided meeting people and was reluctant to look at herself in the mirror. This led to emotional distress and killed her confidence. So, health issues, whether physical or mental, can impact self-esteem drastically.

9. SOCIAL REJECTION

*"Rejection is not a reflection of your self-worth,
but a direction to something much better."*

– Anonymous

During childhood, if you encounter social rejection, isolation, or bullying, it can drastically impact your self-esteem to a great extent.

A REAL-TIME EXAMPLE

Being a counsellor and an educator by profession, I conducted life skills classes for students of various grades. I encountered a situation with a first-grade student. When I entered the class, I noticed a child standing at the front of the class, facing the board as a form of punishment. Worried about her, I asked her to return to her seat. After the class, I approached her, offered support, and inquired about what had happened. To my surprise, she forcefully pushed me away, saying, "Don't touch me; I'm a bad girl; everyone hates me." Understanding that repeated negative experiences could have impacted the child, I reassured her and conveyed to her that she was a kind child and that I cared deeply about her.

In the following sessions, I worked with her to shift her perspective, helping her understand that the challenge lay in her behaviour, not in who she was as a person. I conveyed that making positive changes in her actions could lead to love and appreciation from everyone. Over time, she embraced this transformation, growing into a confident child who excelled in academics and earned the admiration of both peers and teachers.

10. DISCRIMINATION

If you have experienced any form of discrimination based on factors like race, caste, gender, or status, it would hurt your self-esteem.

There was a student from an average background named Suresh. His father was a farmer. One day, his close friend Raghu visited his house to collect a book. He noticed that Suresh's house was small and unclean. Raghu discussed this with his other classmates and put Suresh down. As a result, his classmates started discriminating against him and ridiculing him for his low economic status very frequently. This made Suresh feel very upset and impacted his self-esteem. From this example, you can clearly understand how discrimination can lead to emotional distress, impacting the self-esteem and overall well-being of a person.

Various factors, like how you were treated as a child, your self-perception, or your past negative experiences, can lead to low self-esteem.

Fixing your self-esteem is not so easy and cannot happen overnight, but is possible by staying positive and making consistent effort. You can feel better by choosing to be positive during difficult times, venting your feelings to someone whom you trust, and adopting healthy ways to ventilate your negative emotions in a constructive way.

SIGNS OF LOW SELF-ESTEEM

1. Unable To Take Decisions

*"Indecisiveness is like a thief that steals your opportunities,
and self-esteem is like the key to unlocking the door
to make confident choices."*

– Anonymous

If you are a person with low self-esteem, then often you'll struggle with indecisiveness because you'll doubt your abilities and fear making the wrong choices. This lack of confidence in yourself can hinder your ability to make the right decisions, big or small. You'll always depend on others for every small decision.

You may struggle with indecisiveness in various areas of life, like deciding to pursue higher studies or pursue a job. When deciding about your career, relationships, or making major changes in hobbies, setting goals for yourself, or taking financial decisions.

2. Thinking Negatively About Oneself

"Negative self-thought is like the cloud that blocks the sunshine of your confidence. First, clear the skies within you, and let your confidence shine through brightly."

– Anonymous

You will always struggle with negative thoughts about yourself if you suffer from low self-esteem. Most of the time, you will find yourself focusing on your weaknesses and failures instead of your strengths and successes, and this could contribute to poor self-worth and self-doubt.

Rajesh was a talented employee working for a retail company. Though he was very efficient, he lacked confidence in his abilities and felt frustrated and demotivated most of the time. During team meetings, he held himself back from expressing his views and suggestions, fearing that they would be rejected. He had the tendency to compare himself with others, felt he was not as good as others, and felt that he would never be able to meet his targets. Many times, he thought of quitting his job, but due to his commitments, he wouldn't. When he was offered a promotion and asked to relocate to another city, he rejected it, fearing that he would not be able to take up the responsibility and do justice to the job. His negative thoughts about himself became an obstacle for him to scale up in his career and achieve success, further lowering his self-esteem.

3. Constant Fear Of Being Rejected

"To establish true self-esteem, we must concentrate on our successes and forget about the failures and the negatives in our lives."

– Denis Waitley

You will always be preoccupied with the fear of being rejected, as you lack faith in your abilities due to low self-esteem and self-doubt. This fear of rejection will become the biggest hurdle for you to achieve your goals and manifest your dreams. But it's possible to overcome this fear by focusing on your past achievements, whether big or small, rather than cribbing about your failures.

"The courage to be is the courage to accept oneself despite being unacceptable."

– Paul Tillich

My friend Susie, who attended an interview for the post of biology teacher for high school students, was asked to take a demo class. She feared that she would not be accepted by the students and got anxious. She was overwhelmed with the fear of being rejected, and that impacted her performance in the demo. She was not able to manage the class and draw their attention.

Susie's fear turned into a reality, and the students didn't respond positively, leading to rejection. Susie's example displays how fear of rejection can impact your performance and become the cause of your failure. Dealing with such fear with confidence is very crucial for one to reach their potential and scale up in their career.

4. Prioritising Material Things

"Being materialistic is like gathering clouds—temporary and fleeting, obscuring the true brilliance of life's sunlight."
- Anonymous

People who lack adequate self-esteem may place more importance on material things like expensive cars, digital gadgets, and huge houses than relationships.

William, a successful businessman, struggled with inadequate self-esteem. He had two older brothers who were highly educated and working overseas. He was a school dropout, started a small business at the age of 19, and became a successful businessman when he was 28. Though he earned more money than his brothers, he was not happy. He always felt low about himself, thinking that he was not as educated as his brothers.

To combat his poor self-esteem, he replaced his cars every two years, bought updated mobile phones every year, and used to boast about his expensive things every time he met his family at his parents' house.

He firmly believed that these material things proved his self-worth and success. This might be his attempt to fill the void left by his poor self-esteem.

5. Difficulty In Accepting Compliments And Appreciation

"Embracing compliments and appreciation from others is an artful balance between selflessness and self-acceptance. Embrace the cheers; from within, it lies the harmony of self-confidence."

– Anonymous

Are you finding it difficult to accept compliments and appreciation from others?

Do you find it easy to help others in need but feel very uncomfortable while receiving or asking for favours?

Do you invest a lot of time and energy in others but hesitate while receiving gifts, praise, or compliments from others? If the answer is "yes," then you need to work on your self-esteem.

People with low self-esteem are good givers but poor receivers, the reason being that they feel unworthy and firmly believe that they don't deserve these gestures. I know one of my ex-colleagues who was very generous in giving and never said no to anyone who asked for a favour. She always found it very difficult to accept appreciation or praise from her boss or other colleagues, as she felt she did not deserve it.

6. Social Isolation

One of my clients, Mohammad Ali from Chandigarh, the only son of his parents, was pursuing engineering in the US. He was shy and a reserved person. He found it difficult to interact and establish friendships, and as a result, he felt very lonely and depressed as he had no one to talk to. He lost focus on his studies and needed to submit his assignments. This had an impact on his academic performance. He was very irregular in classes and scored very low on his exams. He got so overwhelmed that he decided to quit his studies but felt very guilty as his parents had invested a lot in his studies abroad. This further worsened his situation, and he completely avoided his parents for 13 days, after which he happened to call his parents and was referred for counselling sessions. During the sessions, we worked together to enhance his self-esteem. Slowly, he started interacting with his classmates, asking for help with his assignments, and making a few friends. He was then happy and started performing well in his academics. So try getting out of your comfort zone and start meeting people.

7. Difficulty In Embracing Imperfection

"In pursuit of perfection, remember that true beauty lies in embracing the perfectly imperfect you. Self-esteem flourishes in the garden of self-acceptance, not in the quest for flawless perfection."

– Unknown

Lisa, who deals with low self-esteem, is obsessed with perfectionism, always setting high standards for herself. She feels this constant need to be perfect in everything she does. Her desire to be perfect in everything she does leads to stress and dissatisfaction. This took a toll on her mental and emotional health, impacting her productivity drastically.

8. Seeking Constant Approval From Others

"Relying on others' approval is like pursuing the shadows; real self-esteem flourishes when you nurture your self-worth from within, rather than relying on external validation."

– Anonymous

People with low self-esteem are mostly found to rely on others to feel accepted and worthy. Daniel, an IT professional from Chennai, constantly seeks approval from his colleagues for every small thing he does while working on his project. This led to stress and anxiety in him as his self-worth was dependent on his colleagues. This could lead to strained relationships at work, lower self-esteem, and impact his overall well-being.

9. Finding It Difficult To Establish And Maintain Boundaries

"Defining and maintaining your boundaries is an expression of self-love; confirming your value is non-negotiable. In the art of boundaries, self-esteem finds its true harmony."

– Unknown

If you find yourself struggling to set and maintain healthy boundaries in your relationships, it would be the result of your poor self-esteem. People with inadequate self-esteem tend to be passive and agree to others' demands and finally end up frustrated and stressed.

One of my clients, Susie from Bangalore, fell in love with a boy from Chandigarh who was well-built and smart. She always felt insecure as she assumed that she was not as good as her boyfriend and feared that he might dump her for another girl. Trying to make him happy, she agreed to all his demands and silently endured physical and verbal abuse without standing up for herself. She eventually married him against her parents' wishes. After two years, her fear came true, and her spouse got into an extramarital relationship and eventually left her for another girl. She got into severe depression and was brought by her brother for counselling. If she had adequate self-esteem, she would have set clear boundaries initially and could have avoided the ill-treatment.

10. Difficulty In Maintaining Eye Contact

"Maintaining eye contact while communicating displays confidence. Working on it is a step towards expressing your self-worth without words, allowing your self-esteem to radiate through your eyes."

I have come across many individuals in my career who are reluctant to maintain eye contact. This may be due to a lack of confidence or fear of being judged. One of my clients got rejected in multiple interviews due to a lack of confidence. He found it very difficult to maintain contact while conversing with others. Even during the counselling sessions, he would either look down or look away.

11. Procrastination

Procrastination is the thief of time.

– Edward Young

People struggling with low self-esteem are mostly found procrastinating, delaying, or postponing things to the last minute, and this leads to a lot of stress. Many factors lead to procrastination, like fear of failure, lack of interest or motivation to make constructive decisions, low self-esteem, and if the tasks are difficult and time-consuming.

My friend, Meena, aspired to write a book on parenting. She was procrastinating for nearly six whole months. Every day, she would say, "I'll start tomorrow," but she wouldn't, as she wasn't sure where to start. She then watched a video that suggested she start writing for 5 minutes daily to get motivated. Initially, she found it challenging, but to her surprise, she completed the book and published it in 3 months. On the other hand, she also sought the help of a counsellor, who gave her some useful tips to overcome procrastination and become productive.

12. Accepting Blame For Things Not Committed And Repeatedly Apologising

One of the signs of low self-esteem is frequently apologising, even for minor actions, and assuming responsibility for things that aren't your fault.

Aneesh, one of my clients, a 9th-grade student, was battling low self-esteem. Sometimes his classmates played pranks and blamed him. The teacher punished him for no fault of his. He could not stand up for himself or defend himself against the false accusations, as he was scared that his friends would avoid him. Instead, he apologised multiple times to escape the situation, even though it was not at fault.

13. Values Other's Opinions About Themselves More Than Theirs

"When you start valuing others' opinions more than your own,

If you are battling low self-esteem, you may place more value on other people's opinions about yourself than your own, and that will lead to stress and dissatisfaction.

Reshma, a beautiful college girl, was popular for her looks and admired by many. She received numerous compliments from others, and this enhanced her self-esteem to a great level. After getting married and bearing two children, she put on weight and stopped getting compliments. This had a negative impact on her self-esteem, and she started feeling very low. This happened as she gave more importance to others' opinions, and her self-esteem was based on external validation rather than her perception of herself.

If you find yourself experiencing any of the above signs, it's essential to acknowledge that you may have low self-esteem and take steps to enhance it.

14. Consequences Of Poor Self-esteem

Lack of adequate self-esteem can drastically affect multiple areas of your life, be it your emotional, mental, or physical health, your productivity, and the quality of your relationships with others.

1. According to research, inadequate self-esteem has been found to be directly connected to psychological issues like depression, anxiety, eating disorders, and chronic stress.

2. It can lead to chronic stress, thereby lowering immunity and putting you at risk of various physical health issues like cardiovascular diseases, high blood pressure, stroke, type 2 diabetes, migraine headaches, skin disorders, and gastrointestinal problems.

3. There are many instances wherein people with poor self-esteem have resorted to self-destructive behaviour like consuming alcohol and drugs as well as self-harming behaviour as a means of coping with their emotional distress.

4. People often resort to inappropriate coping mechanisms like smoking, overeating, and other destructive behaviours to cope with their distress.

5. Individuals struggling with self-esteem issues may withdraw from society, leading to loneliness and suicidal tendencies.

6. They lack the confidence and assertive skills to stand up for themselves or report the matter to a higher authority and easily become the victims of bullying.

7. They fail to achieve success in their personal and professional lives due to low confidence and fear of failure, leading to emotional distress and psychological issues.

8. They struggle to establish and maintain healthy and long-lasting relationships as they may struggle with trust issues,

communication, and intimacy, resulting in conflicts and separation.

9. It directly impacts one's body image. People become too conscious about their external appearance, and this may lead to eating disorders like bulimia and anorexia, which are very common among teenagers.

10. As low self-esteem prevents people from taking risks or grabbing new opportunities due to a lack of confidence and fear of failure, this becomes the greatest roadblock for them to scale up in their career.

Remember, it is always possible to improve your self-esteem by practising self-reflection through journaling and mindfulness and adopting a positive and never-giving-up attitude. Developing a growth mindset and perseverance will assist you in bouncing back from your setbacks and facing the challenges and adversities life throws at you more confidently.

In my upcoming chapter, I will share practical tips to boost your healthy self-esteem.

KEY TAKEAWAYS OF CHAPTER 4

1. Low self-esteem means you don't love and respect yourself. You find it difficult to accept appreciation and compliments from others. You keep comparing yourself to others, feel you are not as good as they are, and experience anxiety.

2. Negative childhood experiences like childhood trauma, which include physical, verbal, or sexual abuse, social media influences, social comparisons, challenges or failures in academics or work, seeking to be perfect always, consistent negative self-talk, and physical or mental health issues may contribute to your poor self-esteem.

3. Constantly seeking to be perfect in everything you do can lead to stress and dissatisfaction, contributing to self-esteem issues.

4. Persistent negative thinking and speaking ill about yourself in your mind, like "Nobody loves and cares for me" or "My life is not worth living," can have a drastic impact on your self-worth and confidence.

5. Practising positive affirmations called self-talk on a daily basis, self-reflection and mindfulness techniques, developing a positive attitude, and transforming your negative thoughts into positive ones can go a long way in enhancing your self-worth and self-image.

6. One of the major signs of low self-esteem is health issues, both mental and physical. On the other hand, physical and psychological issues can also contribute to poor self-esteem.

7. Some of the consequences of poor self-esteem and self-worth include constant negative self-thought and blaming oneself, fear of failure and rejection, prioritising material things over relationships, striving to be perfect

always, finding it difficult to accept compliments and appreciation from others, withdrawing from society, and seeking constant validation from others.

8. Physical and mental health challenges, self-destructive behaviour like self-harming and substance abuse, resorting to faulty coping mechanisms, low performance, relationship issues, stagnant careers, poor academic performance, lack of assertiveness, and negative body image are a few of the consequences of low self-esteem.

9. Self-introspection through journaling and mindfulness techniques on a regular basis, adopting a positive attitude about oneself and others, and being optimistic even in challenging situations go a long way in aiding you to enhance your self-esteem and self-image.

Chapter 5

HOW DO YOU ENHANCE YOUR SELF-ESTEEM?

Follow the following tips to enhance your self-esteem, thereby promoting your overall well-being.

1. STOP COMPARING YOURSELF WITH OTHER PEOPLE

Focusing on comparisons can ruin the happiness of your journey. Instead, accept and appreciate what makes you unique; just like fingerprints differ for each person, your achievements and paths belong to only you. Rejoice in being one-of-a-kind while striving to become a better version of yourself every day.

– Anonymous

Stop comparing yourself or your accomplishments with others. Just like the five fingers on your hand are not the same, everyone is different. Remember, each person's journey is different. If you keep comparing yourself with others, you will never be happy in life. Remember, every one of you has some strengths or potentialities; try to identify them and use them to grow and achieve success in life.

"Comparison with myself brings improvement,"

Comparison with others brings discontent."

– Betty Jamie Chung

One person may achieve success at a very young age, and it may take a couple of years for another person to achieve the same level of success. Comparison with others will not yield you any benefits; it will only lead to negative feelings like a lack of confidence, disappointment, and demotivation.

Rather than wasting your time focusing your attention on others' achievements and growth, focus on your own goals and work towards them. You can compare your current performance with your previous performance. If you have performed better earlier, you will be motivated to try working hard as you know that you can perform better. If you have performed better than before, you will feel good, and this will enhance your self-esteem.

The concept of comparison is unique to human beings alone, and often it leads to negative consequences like emotional distress, low self-esteem, and problems in a relationship.

Have you ever heard a buffalo compare itself with a cow or a donkey with a horse? Such things have never happened in history because these animals don't engage in such negative behaviour, which will lead to their destruction eventually. They embrace themselves the way God has created them, accepting the differences without feeling low or inferior.

On the other hand, we human beings tend to always compare ourselves with others and feel inferior, be it the external appearance, performance, or achievements. Comparison is very destructive. It will lead to low self-esteem and eventually lead to psychological issues like anxiety disorders or depression.

So stop comparing yourself with others, as well as stop comparing your loved ones with others, as this will kill their self-esteem. Some parents tend to compare their children with their siblings or other children regarding academic performance or external appearance. They believe that by doing so, they can bring about a positive change in their child. But trust me, the opposite happens. It will harm the child's performance, self-esteem, and emotional health.

So it's very essential to accept ourselves, as well as others, for who they are and avoid comparing ourselves or others. We need to realise that each one of us is unique and has our own potential. Only then can we lead a happy and fulfilling life.

2. STOP DEGRADING YOURSELF; DEVELOP A POSITIVE ATTITUDE TOWARDS YOURSELF

"Stop putting yourself down. You are your best advocate, and your worth is not determined by the judgements of others. Lift yourself, embrace your strengths, and remember that self-love is the key to unlocking your true potential."

– Cherralea Morgen

Ensure that you appreciate every small achievement that you make in your life. Slowly, you will start making big achievements. If you have helped someone get a job or listened to someone's issues patiently and given them suggestions or advice, appreciate yourself. When you have completed studying a chapter for your exam or prepared a presentation, give yourself credit. If you start appreciating yourself for every small achievement, it will enhance your confidence, and you will start feeling positive about yourself, and this will pave the way for you to achieve greater things in the future.

> *"Success is not final; failure is not fatal.*
> *It is the courage to continue that count."*
>
> **–Winston S. Churchill**

Anytime in life, if you meet with failures, don't lose hope and indulge in negative thoughts like, "I will not be able to make it" or "It's not my cup of tea." Remember, each one of you possesses inner potentialities or strengths and can achieve big things in life. Success doesn't come easy for anyone; you need to be patient and put in consistent effort to achieve the desired outcomes. Develop a never give up attitude and keep working towards your goals. Remember, failures are the stepping stones to success. You need to embrace failures and learn from your mistakes. Failures are much better than success, as they teach you many lessons like adaptability, resilience, and consistency.

Example

You must have heard about Oprah Winfrey, a popular media personality who encountered a lot of challenges and roadblocks during her childhood days and numerous setbacks in life, and eventually, she became one of the most influential media personalities. It was only her determination, perseverance, faith in her abilities, and resilience that transformed her failures into great success. Similarly, each one of you can make it in life. So develop a never give up attitude and work towards your goals consistently, and I am sure you will reach great heights in life.

Similarly, in the case of J.K. Rowling, the author of the Harry Potter series. At the beginning of her writing journey, she faced numerous rejections before her first book was published. If she had lost hope and decided to give up, she wouldn't have become a popular writer.

Let me give you another example.

Amitabh Bachchan, one of the most famous actors in the Indian film industry, initially faced multiple challenges and rejections in his acting career. He tried a lot to make it but was constantly rejected due to his external appearance, as he was very tall and considered unfit for the lead role. Despite making consistent efforts, he was rejected badly.

Amitabh was a man of determination and did not give up. He was ready to achieve his dreams at any cost. Finally, a turning point came in his life: his film "Zanjeer" in 1973, in which he played the role of an angry young man. He impressed the people so much with his acting, and the movie became a blockbuster, making Amitabh Bachchan very popular. After that, he made a lot of hit movies like "Deewar" and "Sholay," and he became a big star.

Despite facing so many setbacks and rejections, he did not give up. He was very determined and confident, put in a lot of hard work, and achieved great success in his life. Today, he is not only a famous actor but also an influential figure and a cultural icon. His success is a clear-cut example that shows that determination, perseverance, and consistent effort can transform failures and setbacks into great success.

So, never give up in life. Consider failures and setbacks as an opportunity for learning, and keep on trying until you achieve your dreams. Remember, even the most successful entrepreneurs have met with many challenges and roadblocks before they reach where they are. We see only their success and not their struggles. Never underestimate yourself; instead, be kind and patient with yourself. Treat yourself as you would treat your friend in a similar situation. Initially, you may meet with many failures and setbacks, but with determination and confidence in your abilities and by putting in hard work, you will be able to transform the impossible into possible and become the architect of your destiny.

" Successful people have fear, successful people have doubts, and successful people have worries. They just don't let these feelings stop them."

— **T. Harv Eker**

Never say "I can't" for anything, as it reflects fear; instead, say "I will try," as this reflects bravery and trust in yourself, and stating "I will" signifies royalty.

You should not allow your fear and self-doubt to overpower you, as these will become the biggest obstacles for you to achieve your dreams. Develop the courage to take calculated risks in life. What differentiates successful people from unsuccessful people is that successful people are always ready to take calculated risks in life.

3. ACCEPT EVERY COMPLIMENT AND APPRECIATION WITH A "THANK YOU"

"Accept every compliment and appreciation with a 'thank you'—a simple acknowledgement that allows the beauty of your worth to resonate in the room."

— **Unknown**

Accepting others' compliments and appreciation with a smile is a simple yet effective way to enhance your self-esteem. Ensure that you always respond with a sincere "thank you" when anyone appreciates or compliments you. Remember, acknowledging others' compliments gracefully will enhance your self-worth and confidence.

When Sugandha's professor praised her speech and said, "Wow, what an amazing speaker you are?" You speak so well! Sugandha immediately responded with a smile and said, "Thank you so much for your compliments!" By accepting the compliment graciously, Sugandha acknowledged her speaking talent.

Also, express gratitude to all those people who have helped you along the way, be it parents, teachers, or friends. For instance, if a friend recommends you for a job, you need to call your friend and express gratitude for their help. Doing this will strengthen your friendship as well, and when you need help again, you will feel comfortable approaching them, and they will feel like offering help to you. But if you forgot to call and thank them for the favour, next time you need a favour, you will not feel comfortable approaching them, nor will they be willing to help you.

4. RECALL YOUR PAST ACHIEVEMENTS RATHER THAN FAILURES

"Instead of worrying about your past failures,
recall your past achievements, and this will make you feel
good and confident about your abilities."

– Unknown

Recall the times when you did well and achieved appreciation rather than thinking and worrying about things that didn't work well. If you want to feel better about yourself and get motivated, recall your past achievements, big or small. Remember the times you succeeded, like getting a good grade or helping someone to solve their issues, preparing a good meal, and winning the competition. This will motivate you and help you see yourself as someone who can perform well in the future and manifest your desires.

"But failure has to be an option in art and exploration—because it's a leap of faith. And no important innovation was done without risk. You have to be willing to take those risks."

– James Cameron

There is no point brooding about your failures. You must consider each failure as an opportunity to learn. There is no success without failure. Even the most successful people you know and read about have met with multiple failures before reaching where they are today. If you want to achieve something big in your life, you need to be ready to take calculated risks. Remember, the fear of failure will become the biggest roadblock to success. If you wish to start a business but are not ready to take risks due to the fear that you may encounter a loss, then you will never be able to achieve your dream of becoming a successful entrepreneur.

When I started writing this book, I was unable to write even one single page a day as I had lost practice of writing after my illness and thought I would never be able to write again. My self-esteem had crashed. I then recalled the days when I used to prepare notes for college students when I had served as the head of the social work department in a reputed college. I used to complete a chapter in one day by referring to multiple books. This motivated me and gave me strength. I asked myself a question: 'When I could write so well in the past, why not now?' I started allotting time every day to write the book and found that as days went by, I became more positive and started writing consistently.

I am sure each one of you must have achieved success in the past, so when you feel helpless or demotivated, think of your past achievements and see the magic happen.

5. TRY TO FIND POSITIVE INPUTS IN YOUR LIVES—READ AND WATCH THINGS THAT INSPIRE AND MOTIVATE YOU

"Enhance your self-esteem by feeding your mind with positive inputs. Read and watch things that inspire and motivate you, for in the garden of positivity, the seeds of confidence and self-worth flourish."

– Anonymous

Ensure you cultivate the habit of reading. All successful people are avid readers. Read motivational and inspiring books to stay positive and improve your self-esteem. By reading consistently, you will be able to nurture your inner potential and reach great heights. Avoid reading or watching negative content like negative news or horror books that make you feel low or depressed. This content will hurt the way you think and will make you very negative.

Now, let's see a few benefits of consuming positive inputs.

- Promote positive thinking.

- Improve your self-esteem.

- Enhance your emotional and mental health.

- Overcome your stress and anxiety.

- Set realistic goals and work towards them.

- Cultivate good habits.

- Overcome life challenges and adversities and develop resilience.

- Enhance your problem-solving and decision-making skills.

- Foster creativity and innovation.

- Foster a growth mindset.

Engaging in negative content like horror, murder, bullying, cheating, body shaming, comparing, failing, criticising, etc., will have a very negative impact on your self-esteem. So, always try to consume positive inputs and avoid all negative content.

6. ACKNOWLEDGE YOUR FLAWS AND FEARS AND TRY TO RECTIFY THEM

"Remember, true self-esteem commences with the ability to acknowledge your fears and flaws and the willingness to alter them. In the journey of achieving success, you sow the seeds of confidence and reap the fruits of success."

– Unknown

You should acknowledge your imperfections and fears and find ways to rectify them. No one is perfect. We are all humans, and we tend to make mistakes in life. But you should learn from your mistakes and try not to repeat them. Only if you acknowledge your fears and imperfections will you be able to work on them, perform better, and move ahead in life.

Imagine you desire to become a popular public speaker but have stage fright. Unless you acknowledge this fear and do something to overcome it, you will not be able to achieve your desire to become a public speaker. To overcome this fear, you can employ various techniques like anchoring in NLP, positive self-talk, visualisation, and deep breathing exercises.

Mistakes are inevitable. You cannot avoid them completely. You tend to make mistakes and learn from them. For example, you missed attempting two questions in an examination due to a lack of time. Then, you have to analyse and try to figure out the reason for not being able to complete the paper, adopt time management techniques, and avoid repeating the mistake. "Crying over spilt milk is of no use." You can't change what has already happened. Never say, "I can't, for anything," as it symbolises your fear.

"You can have anything you want if you are willing to give up the belief that you can't have it."

– Dr. Robert Anthony

Some common fears people encounter are:

- Fear of the unknown.

- Fear of enclosed spaces.

- Fear of failure and rejection.

- Fear of making a loss.

- Fear of public speaking and making presentations.

- Fear of starting a new venture.

- Fear of being laughed at or criticised.

- Fear of getting infected by disease.

- Fear of insects like cockroaches.

- Fear of expressing their views or opinions to others, especially to people of higher authority.

Sheela, an 11th-grade student, aspired to become a dancer. When she gave her first dance audition at her school, she was very scared to face the audience and forgot her steps. She was ridiculed and made fun of by her classmates. She felt very hurt, and her self-esteem took a hit, and she decided that she would never again get on the stage and perform. She firmly believed and accepted that it was not her cup of tea and decided to bury her dreams of becoming a dancer.

Fortunately, during her summer holidays, she had been to her aunt's place. When her cousin, who was a very good classical dancer, heard about Sheela's negative experience, she offered to help her.

She made her realise that everyone, including her, experienced anxiety when she performed on the stage for the first time. She made her realise that by adopting a few techniques, like positive self-talk, visualisation, anchoring, deep breathing exercises, and meditation, by being consistent and determined, and by developing a never give up mindset; she would be able to achieve her dream of becoming a dancer. Sheela, with full determination, embarked on her journey to become a dancer.

She was determined to conquer her fears at any cost and diligently practised all the techniques recommended by her cousin. She enrolled herself in the dance classes. She prepared a daily schedule for herself, started reading inspirational books, practising mindfulness, deep breathing exercises, and positive self-talk. She started visualising as if she were performing a dance in front of a huge crowd and that they were applauding and cheering her. She firmly believed that she had become a renowned dancer and started relishing the joy and excitement of becoming one. This unwavering belief and determination helped her to overcome her stage fright.

Over 5 years, Sheela transformed from a timid girl to a successful classical dancer and achieved many rewards. Her willpower, determination, perseverance, hard work, and never give up attitude helped her to achieve her dreams. She believed that nothing was impossible in her life and that it was solely in her hands to make things happen as per her wish and become the architect of her destiny.

The same thing applies to each one of you; you can make what seems impossible possible and shape your destiny. When you are determined and focused, believe that you have already achieved what you aspire to in life and start experiencing the joy and excitement of achieving it, the universe will align with your thought process and open doors for you.

7. ALWAYS BE ASSOCIATED WITH POSITIVE PEOPLE

*"Good things happen in your life when you surround
yourself with positive people."*

– **Roy Bennett**

Surround yourself with positive people who believe in your dreams, encourage and motivate you, and bring out the best in you. Avoid being associated with negative people who criticise or demotivate you, as negativity can be highly contagious and can kill your self-esteem, making you feel miserable.

Being associated with positive people has a lot of benefits in shaping your destiny. They contribute to your overall well-being. They will encourage and motivate you to set realistic goals and achieve them with enthusiasm. They will always stand by you during your difficult times and provide emotional support. This, in turn, will help you cope with your stress and anxiety, resulting in positive emotional and mental health. By being associated with positive people, you will be able to get rid of your bad habits and inculcate good habits.

Surrounding yourself with positive people is very essential if you wish to lead a happy and fulfilling life, to be successful in your career, and promote your overall well-being. Being associated with negative people will make you negative and drain your energy. So choose your friends wisely.

Let me share a real-time example with you.

Sangeetha, a corporate employee with 13 years of experience, decided to get into the teaching profession as she desired to spend more quality time with her family. She had applied for a teacher's job in a reputed school and succeeded in getting a job as a computer teacher. Her initial days as a teacher were very challenging. The students sensed that she lacked confidence and started taking her for a ride. They misbehaved in the class and challenged her. They started laughing and making weird sounds and would not allow her to conduct the class. Feeling overwhelmed, she walked out of the class and happened to speak to a teacher in the staffroom who was quite negative. The teacher made Sangeetha feel more miserable by conveying that the teaching profession is very stressful and that children are very troublesome and would make her life miserable. She, in turn, questioned Sangeetha's decision to quit the highly-paid corporate job. Feeling discouraged, Sangeetha decided to quit the job and get back into the corporate field.

However, things changed when she encountered the school counsellor before meeting the principal to convey her decision to quit her job. The counsellor heard her out and gave a completely different perspective. She made her realise that children would offer her lot of love and affection. Sangeetha was guided to have patience, be empathetic, and establish a rapport with the children. She was made to realise that teaching is a noble profession, that she has made the right decision, and that she can have a work-life balance and will be able to give more time to her family, unlike the corporate profession.

Motivated by the counsellor, Sangeetha changed her decision and decided to give it a try. As the days passed, the children showed a lot of love to her, and she was able to take control of the class and started enjoying every moment of her teaching profession. The very next year, she received the "Best Teacher's Award," transforming her into a proud and successful teacher. From Sangeetha's story, you can clearly understand the importance of being surrounded by positive people and the negative impacts of being associated with negative people who can make your life miserable.

8. TALK ABOUT YOUR FLAWS AND FEARS TO OPTIMISTIC PEOPLE

"Share your flaws and fears with positive people, for in their inspirations; vulnerabilities transform into stepping stones towards becoming resilient and the best version of yourself."

– Unknown

Based on my 22+ years of experience as a counsellor and trainer, I would encourage you to vent your feelings, concerns, and vulnerabilities with optimistic people. Try to open up with friends who see the positive side of things. For example, if you feel anxious about an exam, starting a new business, attending an interview, giving a presentation, or have some friendship issues or issues in your relationship, sharing them with optimistic people will make you feel comforted and motivated, as they will help you to see the positive in every situation. They will reassure you, saying, "It's normal to feel this way sometimes or to encounter such issues, and as time passes, everything will be fine." They will make you understand that you're not the only person feeling this way and that many people are sailing in the same boat. They will also provide you with some guidance and suggestions on how to overcome the negative feelings and provide some solutions based on their experience.

Discussing your flaws with optimistic people, like lack of confidence, struggle in certain subjects, and being too shy can foster positive conversation, which can make you feel good and find a solution to overcome these flaws. They would help you identify your strengths. Optimistic people are non-judgemental and supportive and will help you enhance your confidence and navigate the challenges life throws at you with a positive mindset.

Sharing your problems and shortcomings with negative people can make you feel more miserable.

Let me share an example.

Ravi, a 7th-grade student, moved from a CBSE school to ICSE as he shifted his house. He found it very difficult to cope with maths and failed his class test. He started feeling very anxious as the final exams were approaching. He happened to discuss this with a pessimistic friend, who responded by saying, "Hey, maths is very difficult. You are going to fail anyway." This negative talk killed Ravi's confidence and made him feel more anxious.

Ravi then met a boy in his tuition class who motivated him by saying,

"Math is very easy; all you need is a bit harder work and practice. At one point in time, I also struggled with math, but after attending tuition and consistent practice, I scored high in math. So don't worry, you will do well in math." This made Ravi feel motivated, and he started working very hard and scored 85% on his final examination, surprising everyone. This is the power of being associated and sharing your flaws and fears with optimistic people.

Pessimistic people are very infectious and will make you believe that you can't do anything right. For example, if you say, "I am not good at swimming," they might respond by saying, "Yeah, you are terrible; you will never be able to swim; you don't possess the skills," which makes you feel demotivated and give up. So it's very crucial to share your concerns and flaws with people who will encourage you and not pull you down, making you feel low and miserable.

Nisha and Rajesh were married for 12 years and had two sons. It was a love marriage. They used to be a very loving couple. However, they started having a lot of fights and arguments because Rajesh got too busy with his work and was not able to spend much time with the family, unlike before. Nisha started suspecting that Rajesh might be having an affair, and it made her very upset. She spoke to one of her friends who had separated from her husband about her worries. Instead of helping, her friend spoke negative about all men, making Nisha feel more anxious. Her friend even told her that she had gained weight and had lost her charming personality and that Rajesh might not be attracted to her anymore and may be having an extramarital affair. Nisha felt so miserable and impulsive that she decided to get divorced.

But then, their families stepped in and guided Nisha and Rajesh to go in for family counselling. Talking to a counsellor helped them understand each other better, get a clear understanding of each other's expectations, and make their bond stronger. They realised they still loved each other and decided to stay together, making necessary changes to improve their relationship. So, listening to negative people can make you feel miserable, but seeking help from the right sources, like counselling, can make a big positive difference and save your relationship.

9. SETTING REALISTIC AND ACHIEVABLE GOALS

"Without goals and plans to reach them, you are like a ship that has set sail without a destination."

– Fitzhugh Dodson

Setting goals is very crucial, as having no goals means having no purpose and direction in life. Ensure you set both short-term and long-term goals and that your short-term goals align with your long-term goals. Every time you achieve a goal, be it a small one, it will enhance your self-esteem and confidence. Just merely thinking about your goals is not enough; you should write them down and place them somewhere where they are visible to you, serving as a daily reminder. Once you are clear about what you want in life, start working consistently towards it.

When setting goals, make sure they are "smart"—specific, measurable, achievable, relevant, and time-bound. Prior to setting your goals, take some time for introspection and understand your strengths, areas of concern, values, skill sets, likes, and dislikes. This knowledge about yourself will help you set clear and specific goals based on your strengths and skills to successfully achieve them.

I'm sure you must have heard about Milkha Singh, the popular Indian athlete, and watched his movie "Bhaag Milkha Bhaag." Initially, Milkha Singh, who was a confident champion in India, faced a setback when he went abroad for a competition. He became overconfident and lost his focus on his goal of becoming a champion. He got distracted and indulged himself in parties instead of practising seriously for the competition, and this led to his defeat. When he realised his mistake, he felt guilty and regretted it.

His coach was very disappointed with his defeat. While he was travelling back to India on the train, Milkha Singh approached his coach, asking him to give him the target to break the world record. His coach hesitated initially, but seeing the determination and willpower in his eyes, he immediately wrote the target on a piece of paper and handed it over to Milkha Singh.

Since then, Milkha Singh had started practising day and night. He sacrificed his sleep, family time, and socialising with friends. Finally, he succeeded in breaking the world record by turning his dream into reality. His unwavering determination and hard work made this possible. He won gold medals in the 400 metres race at the Asian and Commonwealth Games and became popular globally. Milkha Singh's story teaches us that setting clear goals and working consistently, with determination, perseverance, and embracing a never-give-up attitude, can help one reach the destination and make what seems impossible possible.

10. REWARD YOURSELF WHEN YOU ACHIEVE A SMALL OR BIG GOAL

"The reward for the work well done is the opportunity to do more."

– Jonas Salk

In your journey towards achieving your goals, reward or appreciate yourself when you achieve small goals. This will enhance your self-esteem and motivate you to achieve even bigger goals in life.

My client's son Rajesh always dreamt of becoming a school topper in his board exams. Under my guidance, he set smart goals that aligned with his ultimate goal of becoming a topper. He rewarded himself by buying his favourite food, going to a movie, or buying a new shirt for himself when he managed to achieve his small goal. He was very consistent and determined to achieve his goal at any cost. He worked hard and persevered, and that day came when his dream became his reality—he became the school topper and gained appreciation from everyone. So when you start setting small goals and appreciate yourself for achieving every small goal, you will be motivated to achieve bigger goals.

Similarly, if you are writing a book and have a goal to write and publish it in a few months, start rewarding yourself for every chapter you complete. This will motivate you, and you will reach the goal of writing and publishing your book.

11. LEARN SOMETHING NEW

*"Intellectual growth should commence at birth
and cease only at death."*

– Albert Einstein

Learning is an ongoing process; there is no age limit for learning. It is a continuous journey that will enhance your skills and self-worth. The more you learn, the better. Your brain will become sharper and start working better. Learning consistently will contribute to your personal and professional development.

Try out new things, especially learning a new language. This will enhance your confidence and make you stand out in this competitive world. Many good opportunities will knock on your door when you know foreign languages.

Let's assume that you work for a multinational company and you get an onsite opportunity to go to France. You go for a gathering and find everyone conversing in French. If you don't know French, you will get bored and feel left out. But if you had learned French, you can speak to them confidently, which will make you feel happy and enhance your confidence. At the same time, they will be happy that you have taken the time and interest to learn their language. This will help you establish better rapport and connect with them, as well as make your experience exciting and fulfilling. So, ensure that you make it a point to keep learning new things.

12. ALWAYS TALK, WALK, AND LOOK CONFIDENT

"Always talk, walk, and look with confidence. Ensure every word you utter, every look you give, and every step you take should be a strong declaration of your self-worth and unwavering self-esteem."

– Unknown

Talking, looking, and moving confidently can make you feel good about yourself. Your non-verbal expressions are equally important as your words in influencing people and making them like you.

Stand up straight with your spine erect, and when you talk to someone, look directly into their eyes but avoid staring continuously. This portrays that you believe in what you're saying and are being honest. Choose the words very carefully. Also, pay attention to the tone of your voice when you speak. It should not be too low or too loud. For instance, when you walk into a room confidently and say, "Good morning" to everyone during a meeting, everyone should notice you. Speaking confidently makes you the centre of attention.

Remember, your first impression is the best impression. Imagine you go for an interview or a conference. If you walk confidently with your head up, people will see you are confident about yourself. So, when you stand erect, look into people's eyes, and speak clearly and confidently, people will be impressed, and it will make you feel great, and others will see you as someone important. You will get all the importance and attention you deserve.

13. Be Assertive. Learn to Say "No"

If you want to be happy, stress-free, and successful in life, then inculcate the art of saying "no". You should be assertive while communicating with others. Being assertive means having the ability to express your views freely to others, ask for what you want, and say "no" to others when you are not in the position or not comfortable doing what they ask you to do politely and respectfully. Being assertive is very crucial for one's mental health and overall well-being.

"To be passive is to let others decide for you. To be aggressive is to decide for others. To be assertive is to decide for yourself."

– Edith Eva Eger

Being assertive and saying "no" when necessary will enable you to maintain your personal boundaries and self-respect. If you are a passive person and say "yes" to everything, you will always be under stress, and people will take advantage of you. This, in turn, will lead to low self-esteem. It will be quite challenging for you to become an assertive person. But the good news is that it's possible with consistent practice.

To become assertive, you need to realise the importance of setting boundaries and expressing your feelings and needs openly and without hesitation. If you have been saying "yes" to everything for years together, it will take quite some time for you to become assertive, and it is possible with consistent practice. Being assertive has multiple benefits, which include decreased stress, increased self-worth, enhanced self-esteem, balanced relationships, and positive mental health.

Let me give you an example.

Susie, a postgraduate in sociology, worked as a sociology teacher in a reputed school for high school students. As she aspired to impress everyone, she started accepting random work for the admin staff and the coordinators, although she had her workload. As time passed, they started assigning more and more work to her as they knew that she wouldn't say "no." Her workload increased drastically, and she was unable to focus on her work and her family. She began to carry work home and was not able to give much time to her family. This led to a serious conflict with her spouse.

Eventually, the stress became overwhelming, and she got burned out. She was regularly absent from school and received a warning from the principal that if she continued this way, she might lose her job. But she was helpless. She fell unwell. Trying to please everyone, she ended up being unable to focus on her primary task of teaching and evaluating the students' books. Apart from this, there were serious arguments with her spouse, and that hurt the emotional health of her kids. She had no other option but to quit her job. When she decided to leave, the school demanded she pay three months' salary as she was unable to serve her notice period of three months. This added to her stress.

Susie's example highlights the importance of saying "no" and being assertive in communication to maintain self-esteem, set boundaries, prevent others from taking advantage, and avoid unnecessary stress. If you tend to be passive, it's essential to practice saying "no" and assertively communicate your limits and boundaries right away. Remember, it might be challenging for you to start saying "no" and being assertive, but it's not impossible. Be it your spouse, kids, boss, friend, or relative, learn to say "no" when necessary.

14. GET INTO SHAPE—SELF-CARE

"Get into shape; the journey to your ultimate physical health includes shaping your body and your resilient mindset, resulting in a positive self-image and self-confidence."

– Anonymous

Taking care of your health is very crucial to feeling confident and productive. Being fit and active shows that you are disciplined and take care of your body. It's a good idea to exercise regularly, like doing yoga, aerobics, cycling, swimming, or jogging—whatever you enjoy! Spare 45 minutes every day for your exercise routine. Exercise not only enhances your physical and mental health; it also improves your immunity to fight against infections.

Consume a balanced diet; add a lot of green leafy vegetables, legumes, seasonal fruits, nuts, and whole grains to your daily diet. Avoid oily and spicy food. Eat fresh, home-cooked food and avoid junk and processed food as much as possible. Avoid smoking and limit the intake of alcohol. Consume green tea instead of milk tea. Expose yourself to sunlight for at least 15 minutes per day. Also, practice mindful eating by focusing completely while eating, relishing each bite, and chewing slowly. Ensure you spare at least 30 minutes for each meal.

Keep yourself hydrated. Drink at least 3 litres of water daily. Drinking one litre of water on an empty stomach early in the morning will help to flush out all the toxins from your body and prevent diseases. Ensure you drink one glass of warm water 45 minutes after each meal; this will aid in digestion. Also, ensure that you are seated while consuming water.

Have a fixed sleep schedule every day and ensure you get quality sleep for 7 to 8 hours every day to be energetic and productive the next day. Don't forget to expose yourself to sunlight every day for around 20 minutes to get vitamin D, which is essential to boost your immunity and overall well-being. By taking care of your body through a balanced diet, water, sunlight, good sleep, and regular exercise, you will feel very energetic and productive, and this, in turn, will boost your self-esteem.

Sreesha, a final-year B.Com student, struggled with low self-esteem as she was obese, weighing 80 kg. She was teased by her classmates for her looks. She started comparing herself to other girls, who were trim and slim, and her self-esteem dropped further, leading to her disinterest in studies and scoring very low in her academics. She started being very irregular in college and was warned by the principal, stating she would not be able to take the examination due to lack of attendance.

Sreesha's aunt, who had come from the US to stay with her for some time, identified her struggles and took her to the counsellor. The counsellor conducted a few sessions with her, understood her concerns, and made her realise that "It is the internal beauty that matters and not the external beauty, as the external beauty will fade away once the person gets old, but it is the internal beauty that will stay with the person till the end." She was guided not to bother about what other people were saying or thinking but to focus on her health and personal development.

Following the counsellor's advice, Sreesha made significant lifestyle changes—she joined yoga and started exercising regularly, consumed a balanced diet, reduced her digital time, and started thinking positively and adopting a positive attitude towards herself. She stopped reacting when her classmates teased her and tried to be cheerful always. As days passed, her classmates stopped bothering her. She focused all her time on her studies and health. Within six months, she lost 7 kg, her skin started radiating, and she became more confident. She focused her entire time on her studies and scored top marks in three subjects, which was appreciated by her professor. Her self-esteem shot up. Her classmates, who used to tease her, started respecting and admiring her. They longed to be her friends, and boys took notice of her. She made a lot of new friends. These positive changes earned her the title of outstanding student of her class. This example highlights the power of getting into shape, enhancing self-esteem, and being positive.

15. MAINTAIN YOUR STANDARDS

Establishing and maintaining personal standards will help you to establish a strong sense of self-worth. It's important to establish some rules and boundaries as to how you want to be treated and what you expect for yourself. When you decide what's okay and not okay, it helps you feel confident and good about yourself.

You should know that you deserve to be treated with respect and kindness. Maintaining standards will help you to establish and maintain healthy and long-lasting relationships with others and will prevent people from taking you for granted, thereby reducing stress. Remember, when you love and respect yourself and have confidence in your ability, you will attract positive people towards you, who will also love and respect you for who you are. Standards are like having a guide to living a happy and confident life.

Let me share an example.

One of my client's daughters, Subha, completed her graduation and got a well-paid job in a reputed company as an admin. Her immediate boss often stood too close to her, touched her while conversing, and called her by a nickname, making her feel very uncomfortable.

Even though she didn't like it, she hesitated to speak up because she feared that her boss would turn against her and that this would have an impact on her chances of getting promoted. Eventually, other male colleagues started behaving the same way, making Subha even more uncomfortable. When she finally gathered the courage to express her discomfort and ask them to stop, they questioned her, stating, "Why are you reacting so much? You never had a problem when the boss behaved closely with you." Feeling trapped, Subha couldn't think of any way out and decided to quit. However, she confided in a friend who advised her to talk openly to her boss about the situation. The next day, she spoke to her boss, explaining her feelings and discomfort with such behaviour. Surprisingly, her boss understood, assured her that it wouldn't happen again, and warned her colleagues to treat her respectfully. This experience taught Subha the importance of setting boundaries, being assertive, and communicating her feelings openly without fear.

Let me give you another example.

Renuka, a corporate employee, was a dedicated and career-oriented woman who had achieved remarkable success in her professional life. She got herself involved in her work. At the age of 38, she realised that she was feeling lonely and yearned for a family of her own. This sudden realisation sparked a sudden desire in her to settle down, and she enrolled in the matrimonial site and started vigorously looking out for suitable prospects.

Renuka met a couple of men, and despite her accomplishments, she found herself easily falling into relationships that did not last for long. She developed a fear that denying the wishes of her partners might reduce her chances of marriage, allowing them to take advantage of her. Over two years, she engaged in multiple relationships, only to face heartbreak as none of them materialised into marriage. Each time, her partners took advantage of her kindness and moved away, leaving her depressed and questioning her worth.

Renuka felt disheartened and firmly believed that love and marriage were not in her destiny and decided to put an end to her search and remove her profile from the matrimonial site.

She got into severe depression and had to quit her job, making her situation even more challenging. Her self-esteem was crushed. However, fate took an unexpected turn when she reconnected with a college friend who insisted that she attend the wedding of their common friend's son in Chennai.

At the wedding, Renuka met Ravindran, a businessman. They struck up conversations and exchanged numbers, and to her surprise, she found him very interesting and genuine. Ravindran continued to call and converse with Renuka, and after six months, he proposed to her. Overjoyed, Renuka accepted, and the following year, they tied the knot. One year later, Renuka's dream of starting a family came true when she conceived. From this example of Renuka's life, which had twists and turns, her journey from multiple heartbreaks to finding true love and family emphasises the importance of maintaining standards and setting boundaries.

16. BUY A NEW WARDROBE

Let me share with you the story of Sheela, a homemaker who was very busy taking care of her family's needs and avoided herself. One day, she realised that her husband, who used to compliment her now and then when they were in love, had not done so for a year. She felt very low and upset, and her self-esteem dropped.

Her sister from the UK had come to visit her. They went together to the salon and shopping. Both did facials, cut their hair, and bought some stylish clothes, and Sheela replaced them with her old and outdated clothes.

When Sheela tried out her new clothes and looked at herself in the mirror, she was excited and felt great about herself. Her sister complimented her, saying, "You look ten years younger than your age." She started glowing with happiness and looked more confident, and soon her husband noticed the changes in her and started giving compliments. Her self-esteem improved to a great extent, and she was very happy.

So whenever you feel low or upset, try wearing a nice outfit, wear some makeup, and look at yourself in the mirror. When you see yourself looking good, you will automatically start feeling good, and others will start noticing you.

17. GET OUT OF YOUR COMFORT ZONE AND START NETWORKING

"Get out of your comfort zone, start moving out;
in your journey towards success, every connection you make
becomes the road to new opportunities, enhancing your
confidence, and strengthening the pillars of your self-esteem."

– Unknown

If you wish to enhance your confidence and achieve great success in life, you need to come out of your comfort zone and start interacting with people. If you stay within your comfort zone and expect to get a good job or a suitable life partner, it is impossible. You need to go out, meet people, and build new connections. It is very crucial to enhance your self-esteem and to convert your dreams into reality.

Let me share an example of my client's.

William, an MBA graduate, has been working in a consultancy for three years. Though he was a very hardworking and committed employee and very productive, he didn't get the promotion and salary he deserved, as his boss did not like him for some reason. He was upset and, most of the time, cribbing about it to his colleagues. His self-esteem got low. He started believing that he was not good enough and did not deserve the promotion.

William observed that the freshmen who joined after him were given more preference. This made him feel very low. His friends guided him to look for another job, but he got so comfortable in the consultancy that he did not make any effort to try for another job. He aspired to get a well-paid job in a reputed company but was not willing to get out of his comfort zone. Suddenly, his father passed away due to a heart attack, and the entire responsibility of his family came on his shoulders. He had to take care of his younger brother's education as well as arrange his sister's marriage.

He was too stressed and did not know how to handle the situation. One of his college friends, who had come to visit him, gave him hope and confidence. He guided him to attend events and start networking. William started connecting and meeting his school and college friends, going to events, and meeting new people. This made him feel confident about himself.

At one of the events, he met the founder of a reputed organisation and interacted with him. The founder was impressed by him and handed over his visiting card, asking him to come and meet him. The very next day, he met the founder and was offered a very good position with double the salary he had earned earlier. William was very happy; he gained the confidence that he would be able to handle all his family responsibilities well. His self-esteem was enhanced, thereby increasing his productivity. His boss was very happy with his work. The very next year, he was promoted and offered an onsite opportunity to go to the UK, which earned him additional income.

In Williams's case, staying in his comfort zone did not do any good for him; stepping outside the comfort zone, interacting, and making connections played a crucial role in getting a well-paid job, leading to his professional growth.

So, if you wish to grow in life, achieve great success, and transform your dreams into reality, ensure you come out of your comfort zone. Start networking and meeting new people. Connect with your old friends. If they are staying in the same city, try meeting them for a cup of tea. You will feel good and motivated.

18. SEEK PROFESSIONAL HELP IF NEEDED

"Seek professional help when needed. In the journey of achieving success, gaining the strength to seek help from others is a crucial step towards the development of resilient and adequate self-esteem."

– Anonymous

Despite adopting the above strategies to enhance your self-esteem, if you still feel low and demotivated and you realise that your low self-esteem is becoming a roadblock to moving ahead in your life and achieving what you desire, it would be advisable to seek the help of a mental health professional like a therapist or a counsellor. They would help you to gain a better understanding of yourself and the situation and guide you appropriately to gain confidence, take actionable steps, and achieve your goals.

KEY TAKEAWAYS OF CHAPTER 5

1. Stop comparing yourself or your performance with others; instead, focus on your growth and try to become the best version of yourself.

2. Develop a positive attitude and avoid putting yourself down.

3. Appreciate yourself for every small or big achievement you make, and remember that failure is just a part of your journey towards success, so learn to embrace failure as a learning experience.

4. Accept every compliment or appreciation with a "thank you" and show gratitude for those who helped you along the way.

5. Instead of worrying about your past failures, recall your past achievements, and this will make you feel good and confident about your abilities.

6. Read and watch things that inspire and motivate you. Positive input will enhance your emotional and mental health and will help you inculcate a growth mindset to achieve dreams.

7. To enhance your self-esteem, learn to acknowledge your flaws and fears; only then will you be able to take steps to rectify them and work towards achieving your goals.

8. Surround yourself with positive people who believe in your dreams, encourage and motivate you, and bring out the best in you.

9. Avoid sharing your flaws, fears, and problems with pessimistic people, as they will make your situation worse; instead, share them with optimistic people who will motivate you and offer solutions.

10. A person without goals has no direction in life. So, set realistic and achievable goals, both short-term and long-term. Ensure your short-term goals are in alignment with long-term goals and start working consistently towards achieving your goals.

11. In your journey towards achieving your goals, reward or appreciate yourself when you achieve small goals, and this will enhance your self-esteem and motivate you to achieve even bigger goals in life.

12. Learning something new consistently will enhance your self-esteem and promote your overall development.

13. Always speak, look, and walk confidently.

14. Be assertive and learn the art of saying "no" when required to avoid stress and being taken advantage of. Set clear boundaries, both in personal and professional life, to gain self-respect.

15. Practice self-care and take care of your physical, emotional, and social health; only then will you be able to achieve success in life.

16. Maintain your standards and establish boundaries so that you can command self-respect, establish and maintain healthy and long-lasting relationships, and avoid unnecessary stress.

17. Update your wardrobe and dress well in a stylish manner so that you feel good about yourself when you see yourself in the mirror, and this will enhance your self-esteem.

18. Move out of your comfort zone, start going out and meeting people, and make new connections. This will boost your self-confidence and open new opportunities for you.

19. Make sure you seek professional help if needed to enhance your self-esteem, overcome life challenges, and boost your emotional and mental health.

Chapter 6

TECHNIQUES TO ENHANCE SELF-ESTEEM

"Embrace techniques to enhance self-esteem; in the toolkit of personal growth, each strategy becomes a brushstroke, painting a portrait of resilience, confidence, and an empowered sense of self."

– Anonymous

Cognitive-behavioural therapy (CBT) is a psychological therapy and is used to treat various psychological issues like anxiety disorders, substance abuse, depression, and eating disorders. It also has effective techniques to enhance the self-esteem of individuals and make them feel more confident about themselves by altering their negative thinking patterns and maladaptive behaviours into positive and more constructive thinking patterns and adaptive behaviours.

Let me share with you some of the most effective techniques with examples.

1. COGNITIVE RESTRUCTURING

Cognitive restructuring is a technique that helps individuals to notice and change negative thinking patterns to positive ones. It involves a group of therapeutic techniques that are used to alter the negative thoughts and replace them with more constructive thoughts.

This technique aims at cognitive restructuring, not to promote overly positive thinking but rather to foster thoughts that are balanced and realistic. This process can assist you not only in enhancing your self-esteem but also in overcoming issues like relationship problems, depression, anxiety, and stress.

Example:

Isabella is a person who lacks confidence. She chooses to think negatively about herself, believing that she is not as good as her peers. Instead of always thinking negatively about herself, she can focus more on the things she is good at and her past achievements. By gaining insight into how she has the capacity to change how she thinks and feels about herself, she can develop a positive attitude about herself, and this will make her feel positive about herself.

2. BEHAVIOURAL ACTIVATION

When you are upset or in a state of depression, you will not be interested in performing any activities. As a result, you will have very few or no rewarding opportunities to make you feel positive or to enhance your low mood. You can adopt the behavioural activation technique and deliberately engage yourself in activities that make you feel positive or that you enjoy doing, and this will, in turn, counteract your low mood.

For example, let's say Raji feels a bit low as she has scored very few marks in her exam and doesn't feel like doing anything. In behavioural activation, the therapist will encourage her to do things she used to enjoy doing earlier, like swimming, watching a movie, listening to music, or spending time with friends. By engaging herself in these positive activities that enhance her mood, she will start feeling more confident and experience a sense of achievement and happiness, which in turn will enhance her mood and elevate her self-esteem.

3. POSITIVE SELF-TALK

Positive self-talk, also known as internal dialogue, is what you talk to yourself or your inner voice. It makes you feel good about yourself, as well as motivated. It has numerous benefits. It helps in relieving stress, enhances self-esteem, and also reduces the symptoms associated with depression and anxiety. It promotes your overall well-being. It can be constructive or destructive. It influences how you feel about yourself as well as how you respond to life situations. Your inner voice is always with you, shaping your feelings and actions.

Negative self-talk can be very destructive, so try to keep track of your thoughts and replace your negative thoughts with positive ones.

Example: Instead of saying, "I'm not capable of handling challenging or difficult situations," say, "I can handle this challenge by taking one step at a time."

Instead of saying, "I've never done this before, and I'll mess it up," say, "I've got a nice opportunity to learn something new and grow."

4. PRACTICE POSITIVE AFFIRMATIONS ON A DAILY BASIS

You become what you think and say. Your thoughts and words are very powerful in shaping your destiny. So always think positively and say positive things. Positive affirmations make you feel positive and confident about yourself. These positive statements, called positive affirmations, will be very helpful in changing your negative thoughts into positive thoughts and will help in enhancing your emotional health.

Every morning, I make it a point to write five positive affirmations. You can either say these positive statements loudly or in your mind, or even better, write them down. Also, during the day, when you feel low, you can take a pause from work and recite positive affirmations. This will give you instant relief from negative thoughts that lead to anxiety or stress.

Let me give you a few examples:

"I am capable and can handle any challenges life throws at me with confidence." Saying this will help you believe in your abilities and feel confident to overcome the challenges.

"I deserve a very happy and successful life," This reminds you that you have every right to be happy and successful in your life.

5. PRACTICE GRATITUDE

For seven years, I have had the habit of writing a gratitude journal every day without fail, and this has benefited me a lot. It has helped me to think positively even in adverse situations and realise how blessed I am. So, every morning, make it mandatory to write at least three things for which you are grateful. The more you are grateful for what God has blessed you with, the more you will attract more good things into your life. It will help you relieve stress, enhance the quality of your sleep, promote healthy relationships, increase resilience, and promote your overall well-being.

More good things happen in our lives compared to bad things. But our mind is that it always focuses on the bad things, and we start worrying and feeling sad. So, if we start focusing on positive things that have happened to us, it will make us realise how gifted we are.

Examples:

I'm grateful for:

- Good health.

- Good job.

- Good parents.

- Still having a job during the recession.

- Food and water.

- Roof on my head

- Loving sister.

6. GRADED EXPOSURE THERAPY

Graded exposure therapy, also known as systematic desensitisation, will help you overcome fear and anxiety in situations by adopting a systematic or step-by-step process.

If you're scared of something, like being in the dark or small spaces, heights, or even swimming, you can slowly overcome it. Let's say a boy is scared of swimming. First, show the boy the pictures of a pool to get him used to it. Then, take him to the pool and allow him to watch other kids swim. Next, get him closer to the pool and make him put his legs into the water. Finally, take him into the pool while holding him and reassuring him that he is safe. By doing this, the boy can overcome the fear gradually and feel more comfortable with swimming. This method can be used to overcome any kind of fear or anxiety and gain confidence.

7. PRACTICE MINDFULNESS MEDITATION

Practising mindfulness meditation on a daily basis will enhance your self-awareness and boost your self-esteem.

It is a combination of meditation and the practice of mindfulness. It involves being fully focused "on now" so that you can gain insight into and accept your thoughts, feelings, and sensations without judgement. It is being aware of both your internal and external world. This technique generally involves deep breathing and awareness of body and mind.

You can practice mindfulness meditation under the guidance of a teacher or by yourself.

Here are a few simple steps to practice mindfulness meditation.

1. **Get prepared:** Select a quiet and comfortable place free from distractions and sit on the floor or on a chair wearing comfortable clothes. Keep your head, neck, and back straight. You can do this meditation anywhere at any time.

2. **Set a timer:** You can go slow. Start by setting the timer and meditate for 5 minutes; gradually increase the duration to 10, 15, and finally to 30 minutes.

3. **Focus on your breathing:** As you breathe, feel the air moving in and out of your body. Feel your belly rise and fall as you inhale and exhale. Also, pay attention to the change in temperature as you breathe in and out.

4. **Observe your thoughts:** When thoughts come to your mind, both positive and negative, just observe and don't try to avoid or suppress them. Stay calm and imagine your thoughts as the clouds passing by, and watch them float by as they shift and change. Repeat this again and again until you are meditating.

5. **Take a break:** If you find your mind wandering continuously with thoughts of either worry, tension, or hope, just observe where your thought went and try to take your focus back to your breath. Refocusing on the present is the practice of mindfulness.

So ensure that you practice mindfulness meditation on a daily basis for at least a few minutes to start with, as it will help you to relieve your stress and anxiety, enhance your self-esteem, and promote your physical and mental health.

8. SELF-AWARENESS OR STRENGTHS IDENTIFICATION

Do some self-introspection and try to identify your strengths and areas of concern, as well as your skills, values, likes, and dislikes. This will be helpful for you to set your goals based on your strengths and the skills you possess. When you become aware of your strengths, you will feel more confident about yourself.

Example:

Meera felt low at times due to her low self-esteem. She felt that she was not as good as others in her class. Guided by her teacher, she tried to identify some of the strengths she possessed. She soon realised that she was great at organising events and making people feel comfortable. So, she volunteered to organise her class party. Everyone was happy with her work and appreciated her efforts, and she felt very good as she realised that with her strength, she was able to do a great job and gain appreciation. Her self-esteem improved.

You can apply SWOT analysis and Johari Window techniques to identify your strengths.

SWOT Analysis (Strengths, Weaknesses, Opportunities, Threats):

Make a list of things you're really good at (strengths) and things you want to get better at (weaknesses). This will help you gain insight into your strengths and areas of concern so that you can work on your weaknesses and convert them into your strengths.

Johari Window:

Picture a window with different sections.

Some things about you are known to you and others (open area).

Some things are known only to you (hidden area).

Some things about you are known only to others (Blind Spot).

Some things are unknown to everyone (Unknown Area).

You can use this window to understand yourself better.

Example:

Rajesh, an engineer at a multinational company, realised that he was very good at solving technical issues (SWOT analysis—strength). He gained insight into the fact that he had good organising and leadership skills from his colleagues (Johari window—blind spot), which he did not realise earlier.

By gaining insight into his strengths, he became more self-aware, and this enhanced his confidence, boosting his self-esteem.

9. RECORD YOUR THOUGHTS AND FEELINGS

Your thoughts, feelings, and actions are all interrelated. If you think positively, you start experiencing positive feelings like happiness, excitement, and confidence. However, if you think negatively, you will experience negative feelings such as sadness, frustration, jealousy, and anger, and this, in turn, will reflect on your actions or behaviour. You might do something in anger or hurt someone's feelings, which you will have to regret for life.

So ensure you keep a journal, and based on how you are feeling, try to reflect on your thoughts. Maintaining a thought journal and jotting down your thoughts and feelings and how you react will help you to change your negative thinking to a positive one, and you will feel more positive about yourself.

10. VISUALISATION AND IMAGERY

Visualising and imagining the things you wish to manifest in life or the version of what you aspire to be will make you feel more positive and confident about yourself. If you aspire to have a big bungalow or a Benz car, you need to imagine that you are already living in the bungalow or driving the Benz car and feel the joy and excitement and firmly believe that you already have one.

You should not say, "I wish I had a big bungalow or a Benz car," or "I will buy a big bungalow or Benz car in the future." You should say, "I am very excited about living in a big bungalow and driving a Benz car."

Let's talk about Sudhir, a fresh MBA graduate with low self-esteem who faced multiple rejections in job interviews. He felt really down and firmly believed he might never get a job. Fortunately, he met his school friend Ravi at a job fair and related his situation to him. Ravi guided him in using a powerful visualisation technique to manifest his dream job.

Ravi guided Sudhir to create an image in his mind as if he was attending and cracking the interview, getting his dream job, and that his family members and friends were congratulating him. Sudhir started this consistently every day as soon as he woke up in the morning and before going to bed. In two months, Sudhir cracked the interview and got a well-paid job in a multinational company. So is the power of visualisation if you practice it in the right way. Sudhir became very confident, and his self-esteem improved to a great extent.

Follow this to boost your confidence and manifest what you wish in your life.

Set a very specific and realistic goal based on your ability, like becoming a public speaker, an author, or an IAS officer. Write down your goal on a sheet of paper and paste it where you can view it on a daily basis. Before bedtime and immediately after waking up, imagine that you have already achieved your goal or your dream. Firmly believe that you have achieved it and feel and experience the real excitement of manifesting your desire. You need to have a lot of patience. Things can't happen overnight. Many people have given up halfway, assuming they cannot achieve it. So be consistent and have patience and hope.

Adopt the above techniques to feel more confident about yourself, think positively, and be determined to achieve what you aspire to in life. This will enhance your self-esteem, promote your mental and emotional well-being, and you will start attracting more positive things and success in life.

KEY TAKEAWAYS OF CHAPTER 6

1. Adopt cognitive restructuring techniques to identify your negative thoughts and replace them with positive ones, like

   "I will not be able to do it" to "I have faith in my ability, and with hard work and perseverance, I will succeed."

2. When you are experiencing a low mood, adopt the behavioural activation technique and deliberately engage yourself in doing activities that make you feel good or that you enjoy doing. this will, in turn, counteract your low mood and make you feel better and more confident.

3. Use positive self-talk or internal dialogue, which is your inner voice, to make you feel good about yourself, as well as be motivated.

4. Practice positive affirmations like, "I can overcome any challenges life throws at me and be successful," and "I deserve to be loved and respected." This will improve your self-esteem.

5. Cultivate the habit of writing a gratitude journal to focus on the positive rather than the negative things in your life and enhance your self-esteem and overall well-being.

6. Techniques like graded exposure will enable you to overcome your fears and anxiety by facing them in small steps, reducing anxiety and building confidence.

7. Mindfulness meditation will help you to be focused on your present, gain awareness about your inner and outer world, and enhance your confidence and mental health.

8. Gain self-awareness by identifying your strengths and areas of concern by adopting techniques like SWOT analysis and the Johari Window. When you gain insight into your potential, you will feel good about yourself.

9. Maintaining a thought journal and jotting down your thoughts and feelings and how you react will help you to change your negative thinking to a positive one, and you will feel more positive about yourself.

10. Visualising and imagining the things you wish to manifest in life or the version of yourself that you aspire to be will make you feel more positive and confident about yourself and promote your overall well-being.

Chapter 7

NEURO-LINGUISTIC PROGRAMMING AND SELF-ESTEEM

WHAT IS NEURO-LINGUISTIC PROGRAMMING (NLP)?

NLP is the study of how we think and communicate, both internally with ourselves and externally with others. It gives us insight into how our thoughts impact our behaviour. By gaining insight into how our brain processes information, NLP states that we have the power to control our thoughts, feelings, and emotions. We can change the way we feel, think, and behave by changing our focus, as energy flows where our focus is.

Benefits of NLP Techniques

NLP techniques will help you, too.

1. Bring about a positive change in your behaviour by changing your thought process.

2. Improve your interpersonal communication, thereby helping you to establish and maintain a healthy and long-lasting relationship with others.

3. Gain a deep understanding of your inner world, including your thoughts, emotions, and behaviour.

4. It will help you to set realistic and achievable goals and work consistently towards achieving them.

5. Enable you to overcome your limiting beliefs and mental barriers and enhance your confidence and self-esteem.

6. Techniques like visualisation and mindfulness in NLP will promote your emotional and mental well-being by enabling you to cope with your stress effectively.

7. Helps in thinking of alternative solutions to your problems and resolving them.

8. Promotes effective management skills and enhances your productivity.

9. Promotes critical and creative thinking and enables you to make correct and constructive decisions in life.

10. NLP promotes your overall growth in various aspects of life and leads to personal and professional growth and success if applied consistently.

Steps to Follow While Implementing the NLP Technique to Enhance Self-esteem.

1. IDENTIFY LIMITING BELIEFS

Do some introspection or self-study and identify your negative thought pattern.

- I'm not good at public speaking.

- I can't achieve academic success.

- I'm unable to overcome negative thoughts.

- I can't achieve my sales targets.

2. CHANGE YOUR NEGATIVE THOUGHTS

'If You Hear A Voice Within You Saying,'

«You cannot paint.»

Then, by all means, paint.

And that voice will be silenced.'

Vincent Willem van Gogh

Start challenging your negative thoughts and replacing them with positive ones. Changing negative thoughts into positive thoughts and practising positive affirmations on a daily basis is a powerful way to shift your negative mindset to a growth mindset and build confidence.

- "I am working hard and improving my public speaking skills every day. With dedication, hard work, and regular practice, I can become a successful public speaker."

- "I am working hard and am dedicated to my studies, and I can see the improvement. I will adopt effective study strategies and seek help from my friends and teachers when needed to score higher marks."

- "I am working on changing my negative thought patterns to positive ones. I am practising positive affirmation and gratitude and can see the difference in my thought pattern.

- "I am setting realistic and attainable targets and am working towards them consistently. With hard work, dedication, and perseverance, I am sure that I can successfully achieve my targets."

3. PRACTICE DAILY POSITIVE AFFIRMATIONS

- "I am a successful public speaker and have won many awards."

- "I am a very successful student achieving great success in academics."

- "I am a very optimistic person and think positively even in challenging situations.".

- "I am a very successful salesperson and have achieved all my targets."

4. VISUALISATION TECHNIQUES

The power of visualisation is immense. Visualise yourself becoming a powerful public speaker, achieving very high marks, becoming an optimistic person, meeting your sales targets, and attracting an abundance of wealth, health, and prosperity in life.

If you want to become a successful public speaker, you should imagine that you are already a successful public speaker, feel the joy and excitement of being one, and firmly believe that you are already one. Remember, you should not say, "I am going to become a famous public speaker" or "I wish to be a popular public speaker. Instead, say, I am very happy and excited to be a famous public speaker.".

5. USE POSITIVE SELF-TALK

Replace "I can't become rich or accumulate wealth" with "I am attracting an abundance of wealth and success in my life."

"I'm not good at negotiation and sales," with "I am working hard and improving my negotiation and sales skills consistently."

"I can't perform well in academics," with "I am persistently working on my study habits to achieve great academic success."

6. SET REALISTIC AND ATTAINABLE GOALS

Make sure you set realistic and achievable goals and work consistently towards achieving those goals. Remember, a life without goals is a life without purpose, as you will have no direction in life. Goals are goals only if they are put down on paper. So write down the goals and stick the paper where you can view it every day to remind you about the goals.

Take baby steps. Break down your goals into smaller chunks. For example, if your goal is to write a book in 3 months' time and you have been procrastinating for some time. Instead of giving excuses like "I am not able to overcome my procrastination, set a goal like "I am going to write 3 to 4 pages per day or write for 30 minutes to one hour per day."

7. REMEMBER TO APPRECIATE SMALL ACHIEVEMENTS

Appreciate and reward yourself for every small achievement or success towards your goals, and slowly, you will start achieving bigger things. Whether it is scoring good marks, closing a deal, losing weight, or successfully completing a task, if you reward yourself for small achievements, you will feel more confident and positive about yourself and will be motivated to perform even better.

8. LEARN FROM YOUR SETBACKS AND MISTAKES

There is no success without failures. Failure is not the end; it is the stepping stone to success and part of the journey towards success. Even the most successful person must have met many roadblocks and challenges before achieving success. Don't fear failure; instead, embrace the failure and the challenges as an opportunity to learn and grow. Failure is better than success, as it teaches you many lessons like perseverance, adaptability, and resilience.

Instead of cribbing and thinking, "I am not successful in business," look at it as "I am learning and growing from every failure I am encountering."

9. PRACTICE MINDFULNESS

Mindfulness is a powerful technique that will help you to be in the present moment. It is being aware of your inner and outer world. I have been practising mindfulness techniques for several years and have seen a drastic improvement in my mental and physical health as well as my productivity. So, ensure you incorporate it into your daily schedule, as it is an important ingredient if you wish to achieve great success in life.

10. BE SURROUNDED BY POSITIVE PEOPLE

Always be associated with optimistic people who will motivate and inspire you to achieve success. Remember, negative people are very infectious and will make you negative, so stay away from them.

11. LEARN SOMETHING NEW EVERY DAY

Strive for continuous learning and keep yourself updated. Read books, watch motivational videos, podcasts, read newspapers, take up online courses, etc.

12. OVERCOME SELF-SABOTAGING BEHAVIOUR

Self-sabotaging behaviours are those actions, decisions, and thoughts that we create by ourselves and that become the biggest obstacle to achieving our desires or goals as they work against our goals. When you find yourself asking questions like, "Why is this happening to me always?" and "What is going wrong with me every time?" "Why am I not as good as others?" it is likely that you are the victim of self-sabotage.

Example: You wish to become a popular public speaker, but when you get an opportunity, you reject it.

Some of the indicators of self-sabotage include procrastination, conflicts or arguments, oversleeping, indecisiveness, laziness, self-pity, isolation, and self-injury.

As you are aware, self-sabotage will kill your confidence and self-esteem and become an obstacle to achieving success. You need to take actionable steps to overcome it.

Follow these steps to set yourself free from self-sabotage.

1. Through self-introspection, redefine what exactly success is for you, as the definition of success differs from person to person. Set and start working towards your goals, and don't stop until you achieve your goal.

2. Take control of your mind. If you allow your mind to control you, life will become difficult. If you gain the ability to control your mind, you can stop yourself from self-sabotaging behaviour, which will eventually destroy your happiness and success.

3. Share your feelings and goals openly with your friends and family. They may help you stop self-sabotaging and guide you to focus on your goals.

4. Overcome your fears, which are becoming an obstacle for you to take calculated risks and progress in your life.

5. Stop worrying about your past failures and experiences, as worrying is a waste of time and will destroy your present. Focus on the present and make the most of it.

6. Stop getting anxious about the future, as it is uncertain. No one knows what is going to happen the next moment.

7. Stop measuring yourself based on the achievements of others. This will kill your self-esteem. Instead, focus on your past achievements and draw motivation from them to move ahead.

8. Treat yourself with kindness and compassion. Avoid being harsh to yourself when you commit mistakes. Remember, it's okay to make mistakes. We all learn by committing, making mistakes, and learning from them.

9. Let go of things that are not in your control. If you try to control what is not in your control, you will end up with disappointment; rather, focus on things that are in your control.

10. Get professional help if required, especially if your self-sabotaging has resulted in self-destructive behaviour like substance abuse or self-harm. A therapist or a counsellor will be able to help you out.

13. CHANGING PERSPECTIVE TO ENHANCE SELF-ESTEEM AND CONFIDENCE

Follow this simple technique to enhance your self-esteem and confidence by altering your perspective.

1. Select a comfortable place free from distraction and sit in a relaxed position with your eyes closed. Breathe in and out, completely focusing on your breath. Imagine a person who loves and cares for you unconditionally, be it your mother, sibling, friend, or child.

2. Imagine yourself sitting in a beautiful, ventilated room and writing your own story about your past, present, and future, regarding all the challenges you have encountered as well as the achievements you have made.

3. As you are writing your story, try imagining the good times you spent with the person who loves you, how they made you feel, and how they perceive you to be.

4. Try to see yourself through the perspective of the person who loves you. Imagine they are sitting beside you as you write your story, and both of you are looking back at yourself. Put a few questions to yourself. How do they perceive me? What is it that they admire the most in me? What strengths have they identified in me that I am not aware of?

5. Try putting yourself in the loving person's shoes and seeing yourself as they perceive you and the love, care, and admiration they have for you.

6. Now that you have gained insight into how the loving person perceives you—your strengths, skills, and behaviour—try to view yourself through their eyes and shift your perspective. Accept and believe that you possess those good qualities and strengths that the loving person sees in you.

7. Write your future based on the new perspective about yourself. Write how you are going to set your goals based on your strengths and manifest your dreams, how you are going to overcome your fears, and how you will deal with your challenges with confidence.

8.   Now return to the present moment feeling empowered with the new perspective about yourself. Look at yourself as a confident person with potential and talents to overcome the challenges and manifest your desires. You will feel confident and empowered throughout the day.

Try adopting these NLP-inspired techniques consistently and make them your habit; you will be able to enhance your self-esteem, cultivate a more positive growth mindset, and manifest abundance in all areas of your life, be it financial, career, relationships, health, or family.

KEY TAKEAWAYS FROM CHAPTER 7

1.   NLP is the study of how we think and communicate, both internally with ourselves and externally with others. It gives us insight into how our thoughts impact our behaviour.

2.   It states that by gaining knowledge regarding how our brain processes information, we have the power to control our thoughts, feelings, and emotions.

3.   NLP techniques have various benefits, like promoting positive changes in behaviour and improving interpersonal relationships, gaining self-awareness, enhancing constructive decision-making, resolving problems and conflicts, promoting mental and emotional health, aiding in setting realistic goals, overcoming limiting beliefs, and promoting overall development.

4.   Follow the following tips to enhance your self-esteem through NLP techniques.

- Do some introspection or self-study and identify your negative thought pattern.

- Start challenging your negative thoughts and replacing them with positive ones.

- Practice positive affirmations on a daily basis.

- Apply visualisation techniques to visualise that you have already manifested your dreams.

- Use positive self-talk.

- Set realistic and attainable goals.

- Celebrate every small win.

- Learn from your setbacks and mistakes.

- Practice mindfulness and meditation.

- Be surrounded by positive people.

- Learn something new every day.

- Overcome self-sabotaging behaviour

- Change your perspective about yourself to the perspective of the person who loves you the most.

5. By adopting these NLP-inspired techniques consistently and making it your habit, you will be able to enhance your self-esteem, cultivate a more positive growth mindset, and manifest abundance in all areas of your life, be it financial, career, relationships, health, or family.

Chapter 8

POSITIVE AFFIRMATIONS

Positive affirmations are nothing but simple phrases or statements used to convert our negative thoughts into positive ones. You can practice positive affirmations daily to motivate and enhance your self-esteem and to feel better. Practice it every morning and before going to bed at night. Also, anytime during the day, when you feel low or think negatively, take a pause for a second and recite positive affirmations. This little self-talk will give you the confidence and determination to follow your passion and achieve your dreams. It will boost your mood and give you the strength to cope with challenges and stressful situations in a positive way. They make you feel happier and approachable, leading to positive relationships with others. So, ensure you incorporate these positive affirmations in your daily life.

AFFIRMATIONS TO ENHANCE YOUR SELF-ESTEEM

I genuinely think that I deserve respect and affection.

I have faith in my skills and my instincts.

I have faith in my ability to conquer every obstacle in my life.

I am a special and worthwhile individual.

I am incredible.

I intend to always be content.

I possess the capacity to succeed greatly in life.

I am capable of overcoming life's obstacles and challenges.

I let go of the things that are not in my control.

I am happy and accept myself the way I am.

I can overcome the challenges and adversities of life.

I achieve success very easily.

Both physically and spiritually, I am secure.

I am proud of myself and my achievements.

I have a wonderful family and friends as a blessing.

I always choose to be content and stress-free.

I'm content with my identity and my accomplishments.

I make the conscious decision to be in the company of inspiring and motivating individuals.

I've made a positive impact on people's lives.

I am a giver and giving makes me happier.

I deserve everything good the universe has to give me.

I have adequate self-esteem.

I honour my self-worth and treat myself with compassion.

I am who I believe I am, not what other people think of me.

I have the right to a prosperous and happy life.

I love and respect myself, and I have an optimistic outlook on life.

I am resilient and can easily bounce back from failures and setbacks in life.

Nothing can stop me from obtaining my goals, as I was born to be a winner.

I have the capability of making the proper decisions throughout my life.

I decide to work on my areas of concern and focus on my strengths.

I'm working on becoming the best version of myself.

I can pick things up quickly and with ease.

I decided to let go of my past and focus on the present moment and now.

I have complete trust in my abilities, and I am competent.

Everyone respects me, and I reciprocate their respect.

I'm adaptable and willing to try new things.

I deserve to be happy, joyful, and fulfilled.

I have the freedom to design the life I want.

I have the gift of transformation.

I have made peace with my past, present and future.

I have faith in my ability to learn and grow.

I trust my intuition, and I treasure my opinions.

I am getting healthier and stronger every day.

I can draw wealth into all aspects of my life and am a magnet for success.

I decide to embrace self-respect and let go of self-doubt.

I am growing stronger and healthier day by day.

Practising this positive self-talk daily when you feel low and unmotivated will make you feel positive and motivated. Pick the ones that resonate with you, write them down on a sheet of paper, and put them on the wall. Every morning and whenever you feel low and unmotivated, recite them. It will enhance your self-confidence and make you feel good about yourself.

INSPIRATIONAL THOUGHTS ON CONFIDENCE AND SELF-ESTEEM

1. "Always be yourself and have faith in yourself. Do not go out and look for a successful personality and try to duplicate it." **Bruce Lee**

2. Anytime someone tells me that I can't do something, I want to do it more." **Taylor Swift**

3. "Do the one thing you think you cannot do." - **Oprah Winfrey**

4. "You have to believe in yourself when no one else does—that makes you the winner right there." **Venus Williams**

5. "Your potential is limitless. Believe in yourself, for self-esteem is the fuel that propels you to new heights and transforms dreams into reality." - **Anonymous**

6. "I do not care about people who talk behind my back because it means I am two steps ahead of them." **John F. Kennedy**

7. "Set your goals high, and don't stop till you get there." **Bo Jackson**

8. Never give up on your dream because of the time it will take to accomplish it. The time will pass anyway. **Earl Nightingale**

9. "The way to develop self-confidence is to do the thing you fear and get the record of successful experience behind you." **William Jennings Bryan**

10. "If you hear a voice within you say you cannot paint, then by all means paint, and that you will be silenced." **Vincent van Gogh**

11. "Perseverance is falling nineteen times and succeeding the twentieth." - **Julie Andrews**

12. 'You wouldn't worry so much about what others think of you if you realised how seldom they do.' **Eleanor Roosevelt**

13. "The only reason you don't have what you want is because of the story you keep telling yourself why you can't." **Tony Robbins**

14. "Every challenge is an opportunity to showcase your resilience. Let self-esteem be the armour that shields you, turning obstacles into stepping stones to success." - **Anonymous**

15. "Don't give up what you want most for what you want now." - **Anonymous**

16. "Low self-confidence isn't a life sentence. Self-confidence can be learned, practised, and mastered—just like any other skill. Once you master it, everything in your life will change for the better." **Barrie Davenport**

17. "You are today where your thoughts have brought you; you will be tomorrow where your thoughts take you." **James Lane Allen**

18. "Confidence comes not from always being right but from not fearing to be wrong." **Peter T. McIntyre**

19. "The activity you are most avoiding contains your biggest opportunity." **Robin Sharma**

20. "Inaction breeds doubt and fear. Action breeds confidence and courage." Dale Carnegie

21. "You cannot let other people tell you who you are; you have to decide that for yourself." - **Anonymous**

KEY TAKEAWAYS OF CHAPTER 8

1. Positive affirmations are simple phrases or statements used to convert our negative thoughts into positive ones.

2. Saying nice things to yourself daily makes you feel better, less stressed, and more confident.

3. It can also serve as a hidden tool for helping you cope with challenging situations.

4. Practising positive affirmations daily will motivate and enhance your self-esteem and make you feel better.

5. Ensure you incorporate positive affirmation in your daily life.

6. Overcoming your challenges will help you build resilience and improve your self-esteem.

EXAMPLES OF POSITIVE AFFIRMATIONS

- I deserve to be appreciated and loved.

- I possess trust in my abilities and instincts.

- I have complete trust in my capacity to conquer the hurdles in life.

- I am unique and distinct.

- I embrace constant transformation and personal improvement.

- I embrace personal growth and continuous evolution.

Positive Thoughts Benefits:

- Enhances performance and productivity.

- Encourages hope and optimism.

- Fosters an enthusiastic pursuit of ambitions.

- Strengthens relationship with those around you.

Make it a regular habit to recite the inspiring thoughts every morning before you start the day and every time you feel low or demotivated throughout the day, as well as before going to bed. Reading inspiring thoughts will keep you positive and motivated to achieve your goals with confidence.

Dear Reader,

I sincerely hope that my book on self-esteem was insightful and helped you in your journey toward enhancing your self-worth and confidence. Since I am writing a book for the first time, your feedback would mean the world.

Though popular authors pay less attention to reviews, your valuable input can make a lot of difference. Your review will inspire and motivate me to improve and continue my journey as an author.

I would be grateful if you could spare some time to share your review by Scanning the bar codes below, as it will motivate me and help me connect with other readers who might benefit from my book. Every review is valuable, and I wholeheartedly appreciate your time and support in my journey.

"Amazon Review"

"Goodreads Review"

Warm regards,

Shabnam Omer

shabnam.omer@thecounsellingcorner.co

Thank you for being a part of my journey.
I'm eagerly awaiting to read your valuable thoughts.